Reflections *on the* Spanish Isle

The Royal Houses (Casas Reales), Santo Domingo

Reflections on the Spanish Isle

Glories of the Dominican Republic

Foreword by
Oscar de la Renta

JOSEPH L. BORKSON

CYRANO PRESS, *Philadelphia*

In Memory of Marilyn

Copyright © 2007 by Joseph L. Borkson
All Rights Reserved

Printed in China

Library of Congress Control Number: 2006905983

Cover and interior design: Kate Nichols

Unless otherwise noted, all photographs are courtesy of Joseph L. Borkson.

Publisher:
Cyrano Press
P.O. Box 40607
Philadelphia, PA 19107
www.cyranopress.com

ISBN-10: 0-9778016-0-8
ISBN-13: 978-0-9778016-0-2

Quisqueya, divina Quisqueya de dulces recuerdos de ayer,

Quisqueya, pensar en tus lindas auroras conmueve mi ser.

Tus mares, que bañan tus blancas riberas al atardecer,

Quisqueya, divina Quisqueya, tú eres la más bella, tú eres

la más bella flor de mi vergel.

Quisqueya, divine Quisqueya of sweet memories of yesterday,

Quisqueya, to think of your beautiful daybreaks moves my soul.

Your seas, which bathe your white sandy shores in the setting sun,

Quisqueya, divine Quisqueya, you are the most beautiful, you are

the most beautiful flower in my garden.

Contents

Foreword

WHEN I CAME to this country in 1963, a question that I was often asked was, "Am I an American?" I would immediately always answer yes. Obviously, I could see the doubt on my inquirers' faces; so they would then ask me, "What part of America are you from?" I would answer that I was from Santo Domingo in the Dominican Republic. The retort would be, "Then, you're really not an American." I would counter by saying, "I was an American before you were. Santo Domingo was the first city founded in the New World in 1503."

I am proud of my heritage. I have always admired the beauty and the diversity of our flora and fauna. I have found my island to be one of the most beautiful in the world, but what I have admired most and what fills me with pride is the innate kindness of the Dominican people. They are our biggest treasure.

I am so happy that a non-Dominican, Dr. Joseph L. Borkson, loves my country as much as I do. This book will make anyone who is interested in knowing about the Dominican Republic a very interesting and charming read.

Acknowledgments

PUTTING THIS BOOK together was truly a labor of love for me; but the mechanics of doing it, aside from the picture-taking and the writing, were often trying. Of all the people who helped me, I would like to extend a special thanks to:

David Rechtshaffen of Cyrano Press. David was my right hand in navigating the complexities of the computer and in laying out the initial form for the book. My heartfelt thanks, David.

Mr. Oscar de la Renta and Ms. Bunny Williams; thank you, both, so very much for your kind words on *Reflections* and *Glories.* Your words became a springboard to spark the interest of so many others.

Doug Gordon of P. M. Gordon Associates, a special word of gratitude. Doug's layout and design help were of inestimable value, and his attention to detail was oftentimes awe-inspiring. Besides, working with him was always a pleasure.

The good people at US Airways, my flying carpet to the world, thank you again and again. In these times of unnerving air travel, the people at US Air always try to make the going a little easier.

My son, Dan, for his feedback and opinions. Dan's "bottom line" sense of practicality helped me to re-focus when I needed to re-focus.

Señores Leonel Díaz Bomnín and *Leoncio Cruz Montero* in *Navarrete,* Dominican Republic, a special thanks for sharing your expertise in tobacco cultivation with me and for providing the pictures of the tobacco fields in the last chapter.

Joseph L. Borkson

Before the storm (Antes del ciclón)

Introduction

TAKEN IN ITS ENTIRETY, no land is more beautiful, more blessed by nature than that of the Dominican Republic. Warmed year-round by the tropical sun of the Caribbean, yet crisscrossed by mountain ranges which quell the occasional violent wind and temper the hot rays of the summer sun; the island of Hispaniola is a tropical delight which invites the wayfarer to share in the generosity of her natural gifts. There are no poisonous, dangerous reptiles, except in the great salt lake, *Lago Enriquillo,* in the extreme southwest of the country, and there are no fierce felines to pounce upon the unsuspecting; so that trekking through this tropical Shangri-La is a joy to be had without the anxiety associated with other habitats in this beautiful world.

Likewise, the Dominican people are an open, inviting people whose smiles and good humor are so easy to tap into; a kind word or a polite phrase usually brings about an openness which evokes the true feeling of human kindness. A hard-pressed people who have endured centuries of bloodshed and brutality, the Dominican has

developed a way to survive their hardships and still join together in the simplest pleasures of life with gusto. Deeply religious and with strong family values, the average Dominican has learned to balance the basic rules of survival with a generosity of spirit that mirrors the grace and elegance of a bygone era. Of all the glory I attempt to touch upon in this work, the greatest glory would, unquestionably, be that of this unique and special people.

"I swear to your majesties there is not in the world a better nation nor a better land; they love their neighbors as themselves, and their discourse is ever sweet and gentle, and accompanied with a smile; and though it is true that they are naked, yet their manners are decorous and praiseworthy."

—Columbus

For the traveler, a few basic, historical facts are all that are necessary to focus into some of the "glories of the Dominican Republic" which make this land like none other.

Of all the landfalls he made on his first historic voyage in 1492, Columbus chose to begin the task of colonization on this island of the greatest beauty, this land which held the greatest promise of mineral and agricultural wealth. Spain put all her effort into making Santo Domingo, the first port city of the Americas, the capital of the New World and the key and gateway to all the other newly discovered lands. To this end, a great city was painstakingly built which came to reflect the elegance and authority of Spain in the early 1500's. The name of Santo Domingo in the first half of the 16th century resonated throughout Europe as a fabled destination for wealth and adventure: writers and clergymen proclaimed her beauty; businessmen and merchants took heed of her importance and all the princes of the Old World eyed the wealth sent back to Spain from her port. The city became the *plus ultra*, the land beyond all imagination, the new frontier for all cities of the Old World; and in a time when people were learning to read, as Gutenberg had just invented the printing press, Santo Domingo would become the geographical phenomenon of the age.

But, as fame and fortune can be so fleeting, the meteoric rise of the city to such magnificence for the first fifty years of the 16th century mirrored an equally meteoric decline in the second half of the century because of the newly discovered wealth in Mexico, Peru and the expansive new territories on the mainland. This turn of events had the devastating effect of siphoning off much of the vitality of Santo Domingo so that the city with all of its elegant infrastructure, its painstaking beginnings, its great promise heretofore, had now taken a back seat to the mother country's interests as more and more people headed west and south to these new sources of wealth and adventure on the mainland. Santo Domingo and the voluptuous island she came to represent had reached a glorious zenith as the capital of the New World and after 1550, began her unfortunate slide into near oblivion.

Because of this precipitous rise and fall, which I refer to as the Dominican "situation" throughout this little picture book, most of the land has escaped the onslaught of modern commercial development and the people have retained much of the grace and civility of a bygone era. It is as if time had gently spared this island paradise from some of the rudeness and depersonalization which are often a byproduct of modern-day societies. Of course, there are the trappings of up-to-date technology—SUV's, cell phones, the internet and American cable TV—but strong family values and Dominican traditions have managed to hold in check some of the negative influences that these modern-day conveniences have brought there along with them.

Aside from the pristine landscape and the gracious warmth of the people, the Dominican "situation" has left us with architectural treasures from the early 16th century which are unique in the West-

"And, with the added backdrop of the lush, tropical surroundings, there is a special experience to be had that is not to be found anywhere else within the Western Hemisphere."

ern World. As the focal point for Spanish colonization in the New World, the mother country put all her effort into making Santo Domingo and the Spanish Isle the symbol of authority and permanence. Majestic medieval and Renaissance buildings which exist here are different from the great colonial buildings of Terra Firma or the other Caribbean islands of Spanish America; for by the time these latter monuments were constructed on the mainland, the architectural styles had changed dramatically. And, with the added backdrop of the lush, tropical surroundings, there is a special experience to be had that is not to be found anywhere else within the Western Hemisphere.

One of the most magical phenomena of the Dominican "situation" is to walk in the footsteps of Columbus. The one journey he, himself, made into the interior in 1494, from the settlement of *Isabela* on the north shore, exists now, as it did then, because of the lack of development and urbanization. The adventurer of today can follow the same route the Grand Admiral took 500 years ago to marvel at the same vistas of the New World that gave Columbus such grand hopes for this newly discovered paradise. No welcome centers, no souvenir shops, no price gouging the tourists—this is simply a magical trip back in time.

Among the modern glories of the Republic are its best-known exports—great baseball players and fine cigars. Less well known is the miraculous story of *Sosúa,* the little plot of land on the north shore which became a haven for Jewish refugees trying to escape the horrors of the Holocaust. This uplifting story of modern day politics and human redemption brings into focus some of the more contemporary aspects of a country which welcomes its visitors.

Today, most travelers to the D.R. head for one of the many all-inclusive resorts along the coast with their beautiful sand, surf and palm trees; but, a whole country of infinite beauty with a warm and gracious people, a unique and glorious architecture, adventures in history and a very special culture await the more adventurous. This is the Dominican Republic.

Bienvenidos a la República Dominicana

Vaulting in the transept of the church of San Francisco, Santo Domingo (16th century)

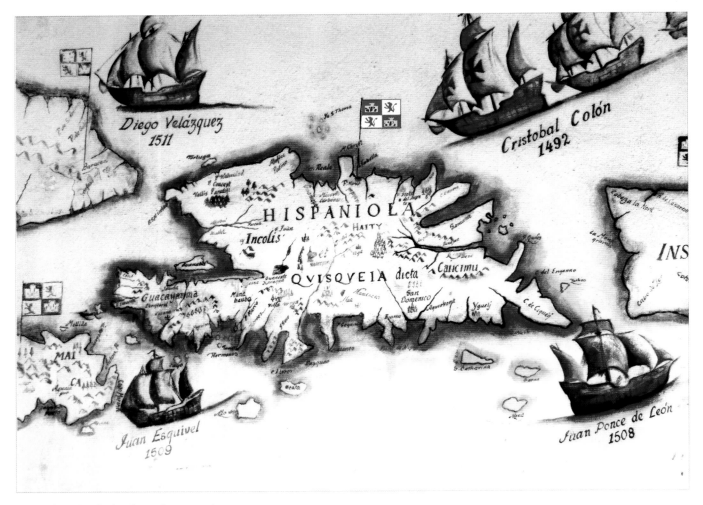

The Spanish Isle (early 16th century)

1. The Land and its People

ON HIS FIRST VOYAGE to a New World, Columbus made the decision to begin the task of colonization on an island which he called the Spanish Isle. He made this decision for two reasons—the land and its people; for although he had sighted land on the islands of the Bahamas and explored the eastern shore of Cuba, it was *this* land, the Spanish Isle, that fueled his excitement and piqued his ever-present anxiety to gain a monetary return to his benefactors back in Spain. He had been convinced that these discoveries were islands not far from the great Oriental empires of China and Japan and colonization was the logical stepping stone towards further exploration in finding a western route to the Indies.

Spain, in order to mark her authority in this new land, built a magnificent city as the island's capital, one which would become the gateway to the New World. Santo Domingo became the port of entry and departure for all ships to and from Europe and the seat of government for the mother country. Here, the building styles of the late

Mangoes

Gothic, the Renaissance and Spain's rich Arab heritage made a unique architectural statement in the New World.

The Spanish Isle, which encompasses modern-day Haiti and the Dominican Republic, was, and is today, a most favored land that often looms as an earthly paradise. Columbus and his men had been captivated by the physical aspects of a land with such luxuriant vegetation, a land where palm trees actually grew upon the mountain-tops, where forests of mahogany and fruit trees grew side by side, where a tall, graceful native population, beautiful of face and form, came to share their hospitality in a spirit of innocence and awe of their strange visitors. The Natives, the *Taínos,* as their mothers had bore them, without clothes and with an apparent contentment in their day to day existence, would become the foundation for what was to evolve into the unique, Dominican personality of today.

The *Taínos* were descendants of the great migratory populations of Native Americans who had filtered across the Bering Strait somewhere around 10,000 B.C. and thereafter. These Asiatic nomads, looking for more land space, eventually came to populate the whole of the Americas from Alaska and the Yukon to the Great Plains and into

The Garden of Eden? A parcel of uncultivated land just south of Puerto Plata

PRINCIPALES RUTAS DE EMIGRACION POR EL MUNDO AMERICANO

The principal routes of migration through the Americas

the eastern half of the North American continent as well as drifting south into the vast land spaces of Central and South America. In retrospect, it was not so far-fetched for Columbus to believe that he was approaching the Asiatic mainland when he saw facial features which looked Asiatic and islands that bear a striking resemblance to the tropical vegetation of the lands of southeast Asia. It is for these reasons that he called the Natives *"Indians"* for he believed he was in the vicinity of the great Indus River of the Indian subcontinent.

The *Taínos* began arriving about 2,000 years ago from the Orinoco Delta region in upper Venezuela. Although there had been earlier native populations some 2,000 years before, the *Taínos* were the first people who had developed a form of agriculture which helped sustain their numbers along with the fishing and small game that was indigenous to the island. These migrations from the South American mainland occurred in canoes over many years by a gradual island-hopping process up through the islands of the Lesser Antilles until they reached the largest island of them all, the land they came to call *Quisqueya,* "Mother Earth." The *Taínos'* strong attachment to this land is reflected in the name *Quisqueya,* as the land provided

Art of the Taínos

9

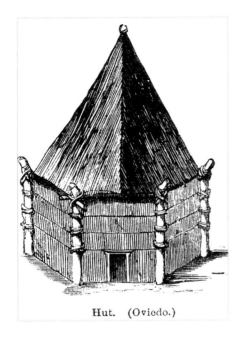
Hut. (Oviedo.)

(Hut. Oviedo.)

Hammock. (Oviedo.)

them abundantly with what they needed. The land nurtured them and they, in turn, revered the land to develop a communal spirit of sharing amongst themselves that was, in great part, due to this harmony with nature.

These *Taíno* natives lived in villages of upwards of a thousand in number along the coastline or among the valleys of the interior. There was a strict division of labor whereby the men were hunter-gatherers and the women tended the house, the family and the small vegetable gardens situated beside their huts. The huts of palm and reeds centered around a *batey,* or central plaza, which served as a marketplace and a gathering place for games and fiestas. Curiously, one of the favorite games was a ball game that utilized a rubber ball from the resin of some of the fruit trees.

The life of the *Taíno* was exceedingly simple: they wore no clothes, except for a small skirt worn by the married women, they had few furnishings or domestic utensils and their daily routine followed a repetitive schedule of the men going out in the morning to hunt and fish, only to return when the noonday heat had reached its zenith and to rest in hammocks made of woven cotton. Drinking a fermented liquid from the *casaba,* cassava, root and the smoking of tobacco were the rewards these men accorded themselves in this ritual, afternoon languor; and the tobacco weed served both as a recreational pastime and as a medicinal treatment.

They believed in superior, immortal beings who lived in the skies with small figures of wood and stone called *zemíes,* which served as intermediaries between the gods and men. It is curious to note that much of this religious direction paralleled that of the rise of Catholicism in the Old World. While the Catholic faith is grounded in the moral teachings of Jesus, the steadfast cornerstone of his teachings is to honor our Father in Heaven; and because the populace of the Old World could neither read nor write until the invention of the printing press in the late 15th century, the gospel had to be spread graphically by way of images of the saints and scenes from the Bible carved into stone. This was similar to how the *Taínos'* religion developed. They had their saints, their *zemíes*, and because they could neither read nor write, they passed their oral tradition on through their sacred *areitos* which were the songs and recitations of their myths of creation and their history. As profound as the reading of the *Torah* or the *Quran*, as solemn and as haunting as the Gregorian chant, these *areitos* joined the generations one to another and nurtured the cultural traditions of the *Taínos.*

To paint a picture of an idyllic native society at the moment of the Great Encounter between the Europeans and the *Taínos* in 1492, is, however, somewhat misleading. The *Taínos* had originally migrated from the Orinoco Delta because of hostile tribes which had pushed them further and further up the Lesser Antilles until they arrived in this land of *Quisqueya*. But time seemed to be catching up with them. Although they could defend themselves against those who would make war, by 1492, their land had been invaded by a fierce band of natives called the *Macorix* just to the east of modern day Santo Domingo in the area now known as *San Pedro de Macorís*. These *Macorix* had even managed to gain footholds further north in the region centered around the provincial capital of *San Francisco de Macorís*. If this were not enough, the *Samaná* peninsula in the extreme northeastern part of the island had already been occupied by the fierce *Ciguayo* tribes, relatives of the most hostile of them all, the fearsome *Caribes.* The Carib tribes, notorious for their ferocity and cannibalism, had made their way up the Lesser Antilles to the island of *Santa Cruz*, now called St. Croix, and had the vicious custom of raiding *Taíno* villages to kill the men, rape the women and take the children as hostages to be caged, force-fed and devoured as their supreme delicacy. For those who romanticize Rousseau's idea of the "noble savage", the reality of some of the native tribes of the New World, unfortunately, was much more savage than noble.

Meanwhile, to set the stage for the Great Encounter of 1492, Spain in the 15th century, like the rest of Europe, had been in the midst of great social and political upheaval. The rural populace lived on large landed estates and looked to their landowners, the nobles, for protection and for their livelihoods. In the cities, an emerging bourgeoisie had banded together into guilds and looked to the crown for support against an increasingly abusive nobility and a decadent clergy which often followed their own self-serving interests. Curiously, in Castile, the central heartland of the Iberian peninsula, the monarchs had no longer been anointed by any religious investiture; but, instead, had taken command by the consent of the people, specifically by the consent of the growing number of city dwellers who were the builders, artisans and bourgeoisie. This evolved into the most democratic system of government within the European continent at the time, and the new middle classes of the Castilian cities of *Ávila, Valladolid* and *Burgos* looked to the crown for support against the high aristocracy who would abridge their freedoms and against the members of the clergy whose abuses went unchecked. The first seventy-five years of the 15th century is an ongoing struggle for power between the high aristocracy and the crown, with the people, more often than not, suffering the consequences.

In 1474, a remarkable event takes place. A young, blue-eyed, blonde-haired girl of twenty-three years comes to the throne of Castile, Isabel I. She is modest, with pleasant facial features and has a delicate way about her. No one expects her in any way to handle the disarray which is so rife within the kingdom. Because of her half-brother, an effete, ineffectual monarch, *Enrique IV,* Henry IV, who has ruled for twenty years and is literally and figuratively in bed with the nobles; she secretly weds the future king of *Aragón*, Fernando I. Aragon was the vast eastern third of the Iberian Peninsula and encompassed the cities of *Valencia, Zaragoza,* and *Barcelona;* and also stretched out to Sicily, Corsica and the Kingdom of Naples, the south-

don Fernando   *doña Isabel*

ern half of the Italian Peninsula. When Enrique IV dies in 1474, she and Fernando come to the throne as one, in a political union that goes on to unify Castile and Aragon in the formation of a national identity. Spain (Castile and Aragon) together with the Kingdom of Portugal are the two European powers at the forefront of this new movement of national identity which will later be referred to as nationalism.

With Fernando's help, Isabel brings the nobles into line by using strong-arm tactics through the reinstitution of the *Santa Hermandad,* the Holy Fraternity, made up of royal tribunals exercising full authority to mete out swift justice against the abuses of the nobles and the criminal element in the countryside. She also sees to reforms within the Church and holds the clergy accountable to their vows of sanctity. Fernando, on the other hand, is the consummate politician. Probably the shrewdest monarch to ever occupy a throne, he was the ideal politician who inspired Machiavelli's famous work, *The Prince.* According to Fernando, there was no greater moral than the survival of the State and his expertise was directed mainly towards Spain's political position while Isabel concentrated her efforts on the consolidation of law and order at home.

I prefer to use the Spanish names of Isabel (English equivalent, "Elizabeth") and Fernando, rather than the somewhat awkward English translations of Ferdinand and Isabella. The English versions tend to caricature their personalities. And, never have there been two monarchs who ruled so well together as Isabel of Castile and Fernando of Aragon.

So, who were these Spaniards who faced the native *Taínos* in the Great Encounter of 1492 and thereafter? Were they as rapacious and exploitative as later historical commentators seemed to paint them? Were they as callous and cruel as others seemed to convey? For the most part, they were like any other large group of men whose initial impressions of the Natives probably ran the spectrum of wonder and embarrassment to the baser instincts of lust and exploitation. They had come from all strata of Spanish society, from nobles and peasants, from artisans and builders to professional types like the clergy, physicians and the notaries. Generally, they were a hardy stock of young *hidalgos,* the second, third or fourth sons of noblemen who had recently fought the Moors and had been lured into the adventure of the New World for the economic opportunity that their elder brothers retained at home as the first born. They were the builders and artisans from the cities who were probably less politically connected within the guilds or the social hierarchies which ruled the towns. They were the farmers who wanted to work their own plots of land instead of working the great landed estates of the nobles back in Spain. They were the idealists, the adventurers and the civil servants who came with dreams of gold, of land and of spreading the Faith. Tempered by years of war against the Moors, tempered by an age which was just beginning to see some resolution in the ongoing civil wars between the nobility and the crown; the Spaniards who accompanied Columbus on his first voyages of discovery were a rugged, robust lot who were familiar with life's adversities and eager to make a new life in this New World.

Spreading the Gospel

The initial direction for colonization and the treatment of the Natives was strongly mandated by the Queen. The Natives were to be treated with dignity and respect, and they were to be instructed in the ways of the Faith. They would be employed in the new systems of agriculture and the mines and were to be paid a fair wage for their labors. Their homes and their lands were to be respected and left intact. The unfortunate reality, however, was the creation of great landed tracts in which the Natives worked in a similar manner as the peasant of 15th century Spain and the social and political struggles between the "nobles" and the monarchy which had been so dramatic within the mother country now spilled over into the New World with a three thousand mile distance between royal decree and the new landowners' interests. This disastrous reality for the Natives had a far-reaching effect on their general well-being. Because of their new, unaccustomed labors and from the exposure to European diseases, their numbers began to dwindle dramatically, so that by 1510, there remained very few Natives of pure descent on the island. The Europeans, too, faced devastating diseases to which they were unaccustomed; diseases like malaria, syphilis and several other tropical diseases that reduced their numbers as well. It has been postulated that one of the first diseases to affect the Natives, and the Europeans alike, was a swine flu which originated from Columbus's bringing eight pigs from the Canary Islands on his second voyage as a part of a shipment of domesticated animals which were found lacking on the island to begin the task of colonization. The symptoms and the incubation period of this flu seem to fit the picture. This tragic unfolding for the Natives, and the Europeans, from the moment of the Great Encounter was, in part, saved by the Spaniards' mixing with the native women, the result of which brought about the formation of a new and stronger race of people, the *mestizo,* the progeny of mixed blood, with greater immunity to diseases from both sides of the Atlantic. The process towards the forging of the special characteristics which would go into the formation of the present-day Dominican had begun to take shape.

While the Spaniard felt a social and political superiority, inherent in any people with a national identity, they lacked any feeling of racial superiority. Their attraction to the native women was real and, generally, not unwelcome by the native women; so that even though the pure native populations were unfortunately becoming smaller; the descendants of mixed blood, the *mestizo,* proliferated. And, the *mestizo* was in no way looked down upon by the Europeans or by the Natives at this time; in most cases, paternal affection and responsibility took over so that a strong sense of family remained.

Yet, tales of horror and misery survive from the first fifteen years into the Great Encounter. There can be no glossing over this pitiful situation. When large groups of people are suffering and dying for any reason, tragedy and feelings of helplessness take over. During the Middle Ages in Europe, plagues would ravage the countryside killing more than half the population; so this was not a new phenomenon in the Old World, but to see it in the New World, this newly discovered paradise on earth, was a painfully dramatic commentary on the "human condition" at the time. To put things into perspective, however, is to understand more fully what part infectious disease played in the decimation of the Natives *and* the Europeans.

The sensationalist aspect of the Great Encounter was played upon as political fodder with greater drama through the workings of the so-called Black Legend, *la leyenda negra,* most notably in England and the Low Countries. The Black Legend was an attempt by foreign governments to somehow discredit Spain and Catholicism in the 16th century. And, why not? Spain, with a population of less than half that of England or France, and basically agrarian at that, had conquered, colonized and explored an empire which was more than fifty times its size and greater than any prior empire in history; Brazil itself is larger in land area than the continental United States. And yet, for all their faults, the Spaniards had been the first: three hundred years before Lewis and Clark, DeSoto and Coronado had explored the southeastern and western expanses of North America; a hundred years before Jamestown and Plymouth, the religious houses of the Franciscans, the Dominicans and the Mercedarians, were sending men with nothing more than robes on their backs, sandals on their feet and the Good Book in hand to learn the languages and customs of the Natives and to spread the Gospel. They crossed mountains, rivers, jungles and vast land spaces, often arid and inhospitable, just to bring the word of Christ to the native populations; and before the English and French had even established settlements on the North American continent, the Spanish had built great cities with hospitals, universities and churches as infrastructure to support them. Along the frontier, strings of Spanish missions stretched into North America while the European mainland remained engaged in bloody, religious wars throughout the 16th century. The Black Legend was the English and Dutch response to such an overwhelming Spanish predominance.

European monarchs used the Protestant Reformation to wrest political control away from the Church and the Bishop of Rome, as

DeSoto and his men exploring the wilds of Florida, 1539

17

the Pope had now been referred to by the Protestants; but in Spain, Queen Isabel had already made great strides to reform the Catholic Church in the 15th century, so there had been little need for any Reformation in the Iberian peninsula and, consequently, religious freedom was much less a motive for setting out to the New World than in the English or French colonies. Religion, unfortunately, had become a political ploy in the new game of nationalisms.

With the decimation of the native population and the rapid development of sugar cultivation early on, the need for labor became obvious. To this end the African slave trade began in a futile attempt to save the remaining native population and to provide the labor required on the sugar plantations proliferating in the southern half of the island. Forts were established along the Guinea coast of Africa as trading posts to which the coastal tribes would bring entire groups of enemy tribes they had enslaved from raids into the interior. The British, Dutch, French, Portuguese and Danes dominated in the slave trade; but the Spanish, who had been prohibited from the practice by the Pope, signed contractual agreements with those who did. The tales of inhumanity and the grim experiences of the six week crossings are already too well known; but, it was said that once the ships had arrived at their destinations, the slaves who had survived the horrors of the crossing had become so relieved to be ashore that they began to regain their spirits and seemed to try to make the best of the situation. They came from many different tribes and areas of Africa with different languages, customs and degrees of civilization. Dispersed to the plantations, slaves quickly learned the language of their masters and began to live a life of day-to-day sameness which tended to override their differences. Still, there were times of the year, after the harvests, when the work was done, that life seemed a little less burdensome and songs and dance from their native Africa enlivened the nights' existence. The fact that the *Ingenio de Engombe,* the plantation mill of Engombe, retains the name of a Bantu tribe from the

Congo, indicates that a feeling of family and community even survived the rigorous demands of slave life on the Spanish Isle. The Spaniard, for his part, treated the slave considerably better than the Natives or the indentured white servants; the slave was considered valuable property and was generally treated as such, although the stories of gross abuses remain. It was also said that the Spaniards had a predilection for the young black women, more so than for the white or native girls, and from these unions arose the "mulatto," the child of a black and white couple. To this day, the term *"negrita,"* little black one, is a term of endearment in Spanish American countries. After all, the Spanish had been exposed to people of color for hundreds of years by way of the dark-skinned Berber tribes of North Africa during the eight hundred year Muslim occupation of the Iberian Peninsula. So, race had now become an economic consideration in the New World and not one of random prejudice.

As the sugar plantations became established along the southern rim of the island, the northern reaches had become less populated and less under the control of the Spanish authorities. Large cattle ranches and an abundance of wild cattle dominated this northern region; cattle from the original stock that Columbus had brought to the island. Because of the Dominican "situation" and because of the lack of communication with Santo Domingo, there arose in the north a ragtag band of rogues which came to be known as the buccaneers; from the French word *boucaner,* to "smoke dry," these men came together in small groups to hunt the wild cattle in order to cure their meat and hides for trading purposes. Renegade slaves, native remnants and the more criminal element of the colony together with English, French and Portuguese profiteers, this "Banda del Norte," this band of men in the north, lived by their wits to circumvent Spain's attempt at government monopoly of trade. Dressed in their stocking caps, cutoff pantaloons, moccasins and wide belts to carry their knives, these colorful characters, these buccaneers, generally led

The buccaneers

solitary lives in the forests with one loyal companion, but would come together in small groups at night to sit around a campfire and talk about what they had seen or heard along the coast or about some plans for an adventurous raid to capture Spanish treasure from the galleons en route to Seville. There will always be a certain romantic fascination with these men who lived a life of adventure and daring, loyalty and self-reliance.

The *Taíno*, the Spaniard, the African and the buccaneer; these are the peoples who will forge themselves into the Dominican of today. The *Taíno*, peaceable, hospitable, spiritual, family oriented, an aficionado of sports and given to music and dance; the Spaniard, robust, aggressive, ready to mix with the native population, tempered by war and privation, bearer of the Spanish language and customs and witness to the Holy Faith; the African slave, with physical endurance, spirituality, hope, and the tribal rhythms of music and dance from their homeland; and, lastly, the buccaneer, adventurous, bold, self-reliant and with a sense of loyalty to the community of the brethren. These are the characteristics which will become ingrained in the Dominican people over the centuries. These are the strengths which will allow a people to confront a history of bloodshed, isolation and privation.

I HAVE ALWAYS SENSED a strong feeling for family among Dominicans and this feeling seems to extend itself into the community, the country and to friends. A kind word and a smile is invariably responded to with good humor and with a warmth that renews faith in the human condition and brightens the day. Once an attempt is made to connect, there is an openness of exchange that no uncontrolled cynicism can shake! In my frequent ramblings throughout the colonial zone of Santo Domingo, many recognize me as a somewhat familiar character who likes to take pictures and keep a relatively low profile; and, yet, even people I do not know by name, will give me a

Quintessential beauty

smile of acknowledgment, a thumbs up or some kind of gesture as if to say, "Hey, man, how are you doing?," in Spanish, of course. This phenomenon allows Dominicans to think of their countrymen as sharing the same circumstances as the next guy so that there exists a real feeling of mutuality in whatever activity they happen to be experiencing together.

On the other side of the coin, because the great majority of Dominicans live at subsistence levels, or below, there is a certain rogue-like quality which cannot be overlooked. Dominicans know the value of everything; the exchange rate between the peso and the dollar, or the euro, is followed with the keen prowess of a New York currency trader. The value of anything from a taxi ride to a baseball cap on the *Calle Duarte*, Duarte Street, is calculated with a precision that has become a way of life. This precision is more than an art, it is how Dominicans survive with limited resources and survival instincts that have been fine tuned over the centuries. It has occurred to me at times that there exists a striking similarity in the day to day life of Santo Domingo and the flavor of life depicted in a signet work of Spanish literature from 1500, *La Celestina*, little known in the English-speak-

Santo Domingo dandee

ing world but a first of its kind in the vernacular literature of the times. *La Celestina* is a play which juxtaposes the medieval values of romantic love, courtly manners and virtuous morality pitted against the growing reality of the baser instincts beginning to emerge within the developing cities. Grace and refinement against an undertow of roguish survival; this often strikes me as an epic, parallel theme in my beloved Santo Domingo, courtly manners with an undercurrent of looking to survive. This is not to say that there exists an element of danger; aside from a minute criminal element, this "pull and tug" rarely takes a conspicuous form of violence, but rather, presents itself in the most subtle and "civilized" manner one can imagine.

The great majority of Dominicans, even the more sophisticated city dwellers of Santo Domingo and Santiago, are friendly, peaceable people who live by a sustaining faith which keeps them going and offers an hospitable face to the visitor. Religion plays a big part in this faith. I have always found it a curiously warm phenomenon to find in

Left: Church in "el Seibo," eastern province
Center: Basilica of the Virgin of Altagracia (High Grace), Higüey
Right: The Savior watches over

the most meager of households, wherever the family unit exists, a small area devoted to images of the Savior or to one of the Virgins with lace table covers and candles to provide a greater feeling of respect and spirituality. Even in families who never attend church or make any outward manifestations of religiosity, the Faith remains an integral part in the lives of most Dominicans.

When they can afford it, pilgrimages are taken to religious sites like the Basilica of the Virgin of Altagracia in Higüey in the eastern provinces; and this ever-present faith is reflected in the human kindness of the people, especially in the eyes of their children.

Language is an especially curious phenomenon within the Republic. As pointed out in the most erudite manner by the great Dominican philologist, *Pedro Henríquez Ureña*, the Castilian (Spanish) language as spoken by Dominicans in the twentieth century most closely approximates much of the spoken word of early 16th century Spain, albeit, with the accent of Andalusia, southern Spain. A great number of traditional expressions heard in the streets of Santo Domingo are no longer heard in the rest of the Spanish-speaking world. This phenomenon is attributable, once again, to the Dominican "sit-

uation," whereby the great effort of the mother country to make Santo Domingo the center of Spanish colonization was rapidly eclipsed in the second half of the 16th century by the expansive effort of Spain to people a world of even greater compass than anyone had ever conceived. The subsequent loss of vitality to the colony and to its subsequent isolation from the mother country by virtue of the great task elsewhere brought about a Santo Domingo that clung to its roots. Innumerable periods of bloodshed and severe economic conditions over the centuries only served to make Dominicans more protective of their cultural heritage, and language, *their language,* was the vehicle which gave them the strength to survive and the cohesiveness during the times of trouble.

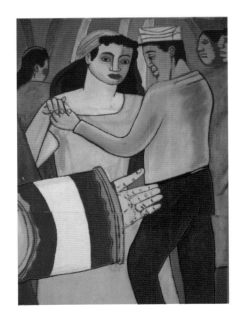

One singular sensation that splashes forth with an especially gutsy, Dominican soul is the music of the *merengue.* This fast-paced, quick-stepping, hip-swinging music, born in the Cibao countryside around the city of Santiago in the late 19th century became a veritable expression of the everyday lives of the poor *campesinos,* the country folk who worked the land. From Boston to Barahona, the *merengue* is immediately recognizable and enjoyable, but for those who are unfamiliar with it and hear it blasted from a low rider on the streets

"La Bachata," by Yoryi Morel
Courtesy of the Museo de Arte Moderno,
Plaza de la Cultura, Santo Domingo

of the American inner city, the impression may be one of complete cacophony. Yet, under the spell of one of those tropical nights, with a few *Presidente* beers under the belt and in the festive company of Dominicans out to have a good time, the joy and fun of the *merengue* is nothing short of intoxicating.

Merengue music, related to our word "meringue," (fluff), is a lighthearted music played with any number of instruments; but the basics are the accordion, the *tambora* (metal strips set into a wooden box with a hole for resonance) and a *güira* (a grated tin cylinder which is rubbed against with a stick). Its influences stem from the *Taínos,* gypsy music from southern Spain and its unmistakable African rhythms. The music, infectious in its ability to bring joy to the crowd and smiles from everyone; the lyrics, simple and in the vernacular, bring out the follies of everyday life, the frustrations of a lover or the physical attributes of some young lady. The words flow like a litany or recitation, not unlike American rap music of today; but unlike rap, the themes are generally upbeat and nonviolent. If American rap has some notable antecedents, *merengue* music can easily be seen as one of them.

Merengue has had a tumultuous history. For years it was taken to be grossly vulgar by the press and the upper classes, but the dictator Trujillo saw in it a powerful tool to promote a greater national identity and used it to serve his own political interests at the same time.

Today, it is relished by all Dominicans as a special Dominican phenomenon and the sheer joy of its music is often spotlighted at

The other Santo Domingo, the movers and the shakers

26

festivals in New York, Boston, Miami, Amsterdam, Barcelona and, of course, Santo Domingo.

Like the upbeat music of the *merengue,* Dominicans are a resilient people; cynicism holds little sway in a country where such a gusto for life is so obvious. Through historical periods of bloodshed, severe economic conditions, political corruption, periods of isolation and depopulation, tropical storms, revolutions and dictatorships; the Dominican always seems to stand his or her ground and smile in the face of adversity. Call it contentment, call it resignation, call it an innate wisdom to adapt to their natural surroundings; there is a certain softening of the temperament to be among people who are quick

Everyday life in the capital. Note the '46 Chevy and '55 Olds still plying the roadways of the capital. Who says Americans don't know how to build 'em?

to smile and invariably respond to a greeting of "what's up" or "how is it going." The noticeable lack of such modern-day ills as road rage and racial tension only add to this softening of the temperament. And this resilience, tempered by the political and economic conditions above, has been forged over the years from the staunch character of the native *Taínos,* the Spanish, the African slaves and that hodgepodge group known as the buccaneers. As stated by an early 20th century writer and physician, Francisco Moscoso Puello, in a collection of essays on the beauty of his country and the idiosyncrasies of his countrymen, *Cartas a Evelina, Letters to Evelyn,* "*Somos una raza sufrida, pero resistente. Le hacemos frente a todas las contingencias de la vida y de ellas derivamos el mayor provecho. Nuestra sobriedad es legendaria, nuestra paciencia no tiene comparación, y nuestra ingeniosidad está por encima de todo elogio. En punto a resistencia, el dominicano retendrá la supremacía por mucho tiempo.*" "We are a long-suffering race, but resistant. We confront all the contingencies of life and from them we derive the greatest benefit. Our sobriety is legendary, our patience has no comparison, and our ingenuity is above all praise. As for our resistance, the Dominican will retain this supremacy for a long time."

Tropical abundance

"The Spanish Isle . . . is the most beautiful thing on earth . . ."

—COLUMBUS, 1492

"Perhaps the most beautiful country on the globe, but in her mysteries, Providence has destined her to be the most unfortunate."

—WASHINGTON IRVING, early 19th century

"Probably no spot on earth, take it all together, and looking at it in its natural aspects, can be found more lovely . . ." "beautiful, majestic, and fruitful in all its natural gifts as when Columbus first discovered it . . ."

—SAMUEL HAZARD, 1872

"Here there are no wild beasts in the forests nor poisonous snakes. You can stretch your hammock out among the mountain fastness in complete security that you will awaken alive and without any harm whatsoever."

—FRANCISCO MOSCOSO PUELLO, 1941

THE SPANISH ISLE is found in the island chain known as the Greater Antilles between the island of Cuba to the west and that of Puerto Rico to the east. The western third of the island is occupied by the Republic of Haiti, from the *Taíno* word "mountainous," and the eastern two-thirds, by the Dominican Republic. A more fertile, majestic, serenely beautiful land would be hard to find; and because of the Dominican situation, most of the natural magnificence of this land remains as it was discovered more than five hundred years ago by the Spanish adventurers. Luxuriant forests of precious hardwoods intermingling with royal palms and fruit trees; fertile plains crisscrossed by crystal streams and rivulets, wide-ranging savannas, the Caribbean's highest mountain peaks whose flanks are covered with blankets of pine trees and the Caribbean's lowest

elevation, the great salt lake of the southwest, *Lago Enriquillo.* Within its borders is found almost every variety of climate and vegetation.

Aside from what might be considered urban sprawl in the great city and capital of Santo Domingo, the land has retained much of its character and natural beauty. Before the contemporary phenomena of urban sprawl and the homogenization of culture in the States, I used to return to my hometown of Jacksonville, Florida, for family visits and would reacquaint myself with the byways and pathways I knew as a kid, dirt roads and paths into the woods of pine, palmetto and live oak. Today, shopping centers and traffic lanes have all but obliterated many of these secret paths that I remember so vividly; but here along the back roads of the Spanish Isle, strange as it may seem, I often find roadways and pathways which have the power to take me back to those sweet memories of childhood. For me, the land is so evocative as well as beautiful.

Two great mountain chains extending from east to west, the Central Range, the *Cordillera Central,* and the Northern Range, the *Cordillera Septentrional,* "septentrional" from the "seven" stars of Ursa Major which is a constellation that always appears in the north, divide the island into characteristic regions. For the most part, the two great mountain ranges seem to parallel each other to create incredibly fertile valleys and slopes between them. The Central Range is the highest of the mountains and effectively provides the country with its two great water tables by providing the source for the great rivers which pour into the Atlantic on the north shore and into the Caribbean on the south shore. From these two principal mountain chains extend secondary chains which add even more character to the topography along with an unending maze of streams and rivulets that nurture the land with its plant and animal life and temper the hot rays of the tropic sun. It is as if Nature had created this special sanctuary for herself and has managed to hold onto to it against the odds, in part because of the Dominican situation.

Following a clockwise arc beginning in the southwest along the coast between *Cabo Beata* and the Haitian border, white sandy beaches with their elegant palms quickly give way to the *Sierra de Bahoruco* which flanks a vast arid land of cactus, agave and the great salt lake of *Lago Enriquillo,* formed originally from a strait extending into the Caribbean. Three times saltier than ocean water, *Lago Enriquillo* is 150 feet below sea level and home to crocodiles, iguanas and pink flamingos. Bordering the northern flank of this low lying area is the *Sierra de Neiba,* a small chain of mountain peaks; the word "sierra" akin to

"Art Nouveau" from the early 20th century; San Pedro de Macorís

Roadside stand

our word "serrated," resembling the pointed teeth of a saw. Moving north from the sierra towards the great Central Range is a sparsely populated area of pine tree forests and a dramatic change in the crispness of the air. The surroundings are fresh, invigorating, and owing to its isolation, conducive to peace and profound solitude. On coming upon the Central Range, there arises *Pico Duarte*, Duarte Peak, the highest point on the island, more than 10,000 feet above sea level. Within a sixty mile distance as the crow flies, we have gone from the lowest elevation in the Caribbean to the highest. Along the northern slopes of the Central Range lies the fabled *Cibao* region and the Royal Plain of Columbus. Here, an agricultural wonderland where yucca, yam, plantain, rice, tobacco, cacao, coffee and more . . . anything that falls onto this fertile soil takes root and flourishes. This is how the Natives came to lovingly call this land *Quisqueya*, "Mother Earth" for the rich bounty it provides. Above the Royal Plain, *la Vega Real*, is the Northern Range where royal palms, fruit trees and hardwoods grace

The delicate flamboyán tree

the slopes and the crests of the mountain-tops so that even Columbus and his men on first seeing them, and already acquainted with the delights of southern Spain and the Canary Islands, were awe stricken with their beauty.

Beyond the northern flanks of the *Cordillera Septentrional,* the Northern Range, lies the coastal plain and the site of the first European settlement on the island, Isabela. Although the area around Isabela supports small vegetation, its fertility is meager in contrast to other coastal plains and strikes a dramatic contrast with the luxuriance of the Northern Range and the Royal Plain. Proceeding east along the northern coast, however, the land becomes greener and more lush with vast sugarcane fields and cattle ranching east of *Puerto Plata,* rice paddies in the vicinity of *Nagua* and great numbers of wild palms on the *Samaná* peninsula. There are probably more palm trees per square mile around *Samaná* than any other place in the world and in the Spring, the great humpback whales from the cold

The flower of the flamboyán, fallen onto the roadway

waters of the North Atlantic migrate here to breed in the warm Bay of *Samaná.* Crossing the Bay of *Samaná* one encounters an area of few roads, prehistoric caves and low-lying fields of tropical vegetation. The eastern shore is sparsely populated with rich agricultural tracts, cattle ranches and further south, the resorts of Punta Cana and Casa de Campo. Midway between these two elegant resorts in the eastern provinces, near the little town of *San Rafael de Yuma* lies the fortress-like palace of *Juan Ponce de León,* built in 1508. Perhaps the most surreal vision on the island, a stately, late medieval, early Renaissance edifice stands with an authoritarian air among fields of sugarcane. Moving west along the southern shore, bathed by the waters of the Caribbean, the landscape alternates between vast expanses of cattle ranches, drier regions of scrub and more lush areas centered around the rivers which empty into the Caribbean until we return to Santo Domingo. West of the city along the shore lies

Patio of the Tostado House (Casa del Tostado), Santo Domingo

an exceptionally rich and luxuriant land near the towns of *San Cristóbal* and *Baní* and once again we find ourselves in the land of cactus and agave in our return towards the *Hoya de Enriquillo*, the valley between the Sierras Bahoruco and Neiba. The interior of the Spanish Isle with its mountain streams and rivulets create incredible regions of agricultural fertility, expansive savannas, large areas of pine forests, formidable mountain ranges and rain forests which delight the senses with their pristine beauty. Taken in its entirety,

35

Samaná

Quisqueya, "Mother Earth," does indeed take care of her children with bountiful blessings from the heart.

Although the title of this chapter is "The Land and its People," in a sense, it is often difficult to separate the land from the people. The great majority of Dominicans live so close to the land, so in tune with her harvests and her planting times that the land and the people almost appear as one at times, unable to be pulled apart one from the other. There is such an intimacy between the two that I often think of how the land has molded the Dominican personality, that *geographical determinism* fulfilling its mission, and about how the people have become so much a part of the land they care for.

From out of it all has emerged today's Dominican, strong, resilient, intimate with his/her surroundings and with a hospitality that comes from the bountiful nurturing of the land for so many years. The history of wars and bloodshed, the periods of economic privation and the periods of isolation from the mother country have only served to toughen the Dominican of today so that he/she has learned well enough the lessons of survival and how to make do with whatever the circumstance, and, to rise above it all with that special gusto for life that is uniquely Dominican.

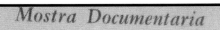

Mostra Documentaria
CRISTOFORO COLOMBO IL GENOVESE
L'intuito e l'ardimento al servizio dell'umanità

Enti Organizzatori

MINISTERO PER I BENI CULTURALI E AMBIENTALI

COMITATO NAZIONALE PER LE CELEBRAZIONI DEL V CENTENARIO DELLA SCOPERTA DELL'AMERICA

COMUNE DI GENOVA

ISTITUTO POLIGRAFICO E ZECCA DELLO STATO

Consulenza Scientifica

PAOLO EMILIO TAVIANI

Curatori

SIMONETTA CONTI - GIORGIO BENVENUTI

ANGIOLA FERRO - ANDREA PALADINI

Designer

FRANCESCO PIRELLA

2. Columbus

An age will come after many years when the Ocean will loose the chains of things, and a huge land lie revealed; when Thiphys (Jason's pilot) will disclose new worlds and Thule (Iceland) no more be the ultimate.

—SENECA, *MEDEA* (1st century A.D.)

CRISTOFORO COLOMBO was an extraordinary man whose vision and determination changed the course of modern history. Few men in history, or women for that matter, have risen from such humble beginnings to overcome such tremendous odds and accomplish such monumental deeds. Yet his story and the events of his time have more often than not been shrouded in shadow and misunderstanding. His story and the magnificent adventure of his discoveries when seen in true historical perspective, reflect a nobility of the human spirit and a precious glimpse into the exciting times in which he lived.

Many have asked me what this fascination with the figure of Columbus is all about. There are those, who aside from disinterest, also look to discredit his accomplishments because of some political or individual agenda. It would seem that the man has as many detractors five hundred years after the fact as he had in life.

To me, I see a man whose humble beginnings did not predispose him to any greatness, a human being born into a rigid, hierarchical

society which put little value on the rights or dignity of the individual and who rose to greatness despite the odds; yet it is here, in his childhood and his growing into manhood, that the seed of his greatness was sown. Without any formal education, he was completely self-taught in reading, writing, business-like manners, navigation and languages. He learned because he wanted to learn. Every endeavor that he undertook, he extracted as much useful knowledge as he could with a mind that knew no barriers. The story of his life has as much adventure as any Robert Louis Stevenson novel and his keen sense of observation places him as an ideal figure of the Renaissance. To him, geographical knowledge was tantamount to knowledge itself. To understand where one is in life and to see that position in relation to one's surroundings is a powerful tool to knowledge in general. I, myself, who love to travel, feel so much at a loss without the aid of a good map; and it is this relation to place that helps me to identify and relate to my travels. Many have written theories about *geographical determinism;* that is, how the environment affects activity, industry, even personality itself. And yet, when we come to know a place well, the answers to so many questions become so much clearer.

He was devoted to his wife and sons, to his Queen, to the noble city of his birth and most of all, he was steadfast in his faith towards the Almighty. He treated all people with respect, regardless of their social position, and only became vexed by the ignorant who jeered him or by the highly educated who looked upon him with disdain. This devotion shows itself in so many ways, but a good indication can be seen in the order in which he names the landfalls on his first voyage: the first island he discovers, he calls San Salvador after his Savior; the second, Isabela after his Queen; the third, Fernandina after the King; the fourth, Juana (Cuba) after the *Infanta* (the princess) and the fifth, and most promising of all, the Spanish Isle, the present-day Dominican Republic. Under his direction, the Spanish Isle was to become the centerpiece for Spain's colonization and the base for all further exploration into the newly discovered lands. Isabela, and shortly thereafter, Santo Domingo, became the most famous towns of the New World; and this is why his name is so intimately linked with the Spanish Isle.

Samuel Eliot Morison, a Harvard professor in nautical studies, wrote a Pulitzer Prize winning book on the life of Columbus, entitled *Admiral of the Ocean Sea,* in the early 1940s. A fascinating account of Columbus's life pieced together by actual notarial records of the time, Morison virtually recreates the great discovery by following the voyages himself with a small crew in the same type of vessels; he also used the same instruments of navigation and experienced the currents, weather conditions and landfalls firsthand that Columbus had encountered 450 years before. And, he chronicles it all in the above mentioned book.

By the way, the profession of notary in Columbus's time was much different from what it is today. Today, a notary confirms the signature and the identification of the signer; but back then, a notary was a pillar of the community who drew up business contracts, bills of sale, real estate claims, etc., which were usually written in Latin and which did not bear the signatures of the parties concerned. As most of the populace could neither read nor write, this was a very important profession and served as the definitive word in a court of law. Being a notary was generally passed from father to son as there were well known families who followed the trade; and when a family line died out for any reason, the records were usually given over to the municipal archives to remain as legal testaments in perpetuity. These are the documents perused by Morison to create his masterpiece.

COLUMBUS WAS BORN in Genoa, 1451, to Domenico Colombo and Susanna Fontanarossa. His father Domenico was a master weaver; one who owned his own looms, bought his own wool, sold the finished cloth and taught apprentice boys their trade. This placed

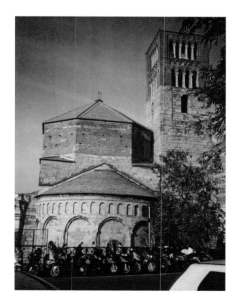

San Stefano, the church in which Columbus was baptized, Genoa

him respectably in the lower middle class and secured his membership in the local guild of clothiers. His father was a likable fellow, optimistic and easy to get along with; but there were times when he would make promises that he was unable to keep and buy goods for which he was unable to pay. He was the kind of man who when business was slack, would take the boys fishing. After establishing himself as a clothier, he sidelined his woolen trade and started a wine and cheese business in which he would often become his best customer.

As I pass through the winding streets and alleyways *(i carruggi)* of Genoa's old town, I am struck by the mystery and intrigue which seem pervasive. The streets branch into hundreds of narrow alleyways, which owing to the tenements' rising some six to eight stories on either side, completely obliterate the sun so that even at high noon in the middle of summer, the alleyways quickly become pitch black and to anyone who is not a part of the neighborhood offer a dangerous way to go. I have never experienced anything like this in any other city or town I have come to know. At the same time, as Italy's largest port, Genoa is alive with people from all over the world: Africans in native dress, merchants from the Middle East and the Orient, all

15th century Genoa. Note the breakwater and the old town's center on the eastern side of the port. Much of it remains today as it was then.

classes of Europeans and even Spanish-speaking people from Central and South America; anyone who has come to know the Seven Seas. I can almost picture a little Christopher, having received a few coins and a glass of wine from his father on the occasion of his Saint's Day, wandering through these tiny streets to contemplate all the things he could buy with his newly acquired wealth or possibly choosing to save his coins instead. With goods from all corners of the known world, he would have had a hard time choosing: some insignificant little map or handwritten parchment, a small compass or maybe a ship's model. How his mind must have raced through the possibilities! The appearance of the old town today has probably changed very little from the 15th century Genoa of Columbus's time.

The tiny streets of old Genoa

Genoa's maritime prowess came to the fore during the Crusades. Genovese ships and Genovese mariners transported the Crusaders to and from the Holy Land across the sea that became their special domain. When the Crusades ended, the Genovese became experts in the shipment of goods throughout the region with trading outposts along the coasts of the Mediterranean, the Black Sea, Spain, Portugal and the coast of West Africa. Business was the language they spoke and they spoke or dealt with little else. There was an economy of language so that they spoke just enough to agree to the terms; very little socialization went along with the business. If they were not direct traders, they often served as factors, financiers, through the famous Bank of Saint George, *il Banco di San Giorgio,* the institution that became synonymous with the power and wealth of the city itself. In time Genoa practically controlled the Mediterranean by developing market monopolies throughout the region and came to be called *Genova, la Superba,* Genoa, the Proud, by Petrarch in the 14th century because of the magnificent palaces built by the ruling families in this lucrative maritime trade.

The famous Bank of St. George; port in Genoa

The ruling families divided the clustered network of alleyways into their own turfs so that the social and political order was reflected

Columbus learned to sail in a small craft like this one

in the tangled structure of its residential areas. To be loyal and well connected to one of these ruling families was an absolute necessity to success in 14th and 15th century Genoa and to be familiar with this social fabric is crucial to understanding the character of Columbus, affable and political, as much as his conscience and passion would allow.

Young Christopher learned the value of hard work at an early age and developed a head for business. He and his younger brother were responsible for carding the raw wool that their father had bought, while his mother spun it into yarn. They then prepared it for the dyeing process and prepared it to be woven on the loom. What little spare time to be had on a Sunday or a feast day would be spent learning to navigate the sea along the Genovese coastline in a small, one-man sailboat. Many a Genovese young man would learn the ways of the sea as this was the important skill that would help him to position his future in the maritime trade, the center of Genovese life; and young Christopher learned to sail along the coast from Genoa to Portofino in the east and from Genoa to Savona in the west. This is the sun-drenched area we refer to today as the Italian Riviera. In 1470, at the

The old and the new co-mingle in the old port of Genoa

age of about 19 years old, having reached his maturity according to Genovese law, he put his name to a debt of wines delivered to his father and began to establish his reputation for being a somewhat better security risk than Domenico as a hardworking, no nonsense young man with a future.

During the early 1470's, he is sent to the island of Chios in the Aegean by one of the ruling families who had an interest in the cultivation and trade of mastic. Mastic, related to our word *masticate,* to chew, is derived from the resin of a tree which only grows in the southern part of this Greek island and was thought to have medicinal qualities at the time. A great trade throughout the Mediterranean littoral grew out of the mastic trade and the Genovese built palaces and whole fortified communities on the island to protect their interests from the Turks, and any other privateers, who would try to muscle into this lucrative trade. Columbus may have spent close to two years at Chios while expanding his navigational skills in the eastern Mediterranean and representing the keen business interests of his compatriots in the exploitation of mastic. This took some remarkable maneuvering considering that Chios is an island within five miles of the Turkish mainland.

Mastic tree, the mastic villages and a Genovese palace on the Greek island of Chios in the Aegean

In 1476, when most of the Mediterranean nations were at war, Columbus signed up for a Genovese convoy bound with a load of Chian mastic for ports in Lisbon, England and the Netherlands. The group of five ships made its way through the straits of Gibraltar and was proceeding up the southern coast of Portugal when it was attacked by a Franco-Portuguese fleet of thirteen warships. A day-long battle ensued with fierce fighting on both sides. Three of the Genovese ships went down and four of the enemies'. Columbus had fought on one of the ships that went down and even though he was wounded, he jumped into the sea, grabbed hold of one of the ship's planks and pushed himself ahead to reach the shore, over six miles distant. The townspeople of the little seacoast town treated all surviving mariners kindly and when he had regained some of his strength, he made his way by land to Lisbon and was taken in by the Genovese community which had situated itself within the port area of the city. It was here that destiny awaited him.

Lisbon had become the world center for oceanic voyaging and discovery in the last half of the 15th century. The Portuguese had made themselves the most progressive and liveliest country in Europe. Here, he found himself among people who could teach him all he was eager to learn: the Portuguese and Castilian languages, the new *linguae francae* of the maritime trade; Latin to study the geographical works of antiquity; mathematics and astronomy to hone his skills in navigation; shipbuilding and rigging; and the spirit and angst for further discovery. The Genovese served the Portuguese well with their special talents in map making and Columbus worked together with his brother Bartholomew, who had previously arrived in Lisbon, in this craft of drawing up maps. The Portuguese were anxious to chart their new colonial possessions in the Atlantic and along the west coast of Africa so that map making was an important activity to their far-reaching adventures. After a short time, eager to return to the sea, Columbus chose to ship out on a trading voyage from Lisbon to the

Azores, and from there, to Bristol (England) and up to Iceland. In all his adventures, he seemed to absorb knowledge like a sponge. Everywhere he went he observed the ocean, the wind currents and the seasonal conditions to his destinations. Shortly after his Icelandic voyage, he shipped out to the west coast of Africa under Genovese patronage and brilliantly deduced that **if he wanted to sail west into the ocean sea, the winds and the currents were more favorable in the southern latitudes, while the northern latitudes would serve him better on a return voyage.** This was no small deduction as it took months, maybe years, for him to piece this information together from his voyages to Iceland and the African coast; and only with an astute eye towards Nature's secrets did he come to understand the trade winds and their relation to that great unknown we now call the Atlantic Ocean.

With his rudimentary knowledge of Latin, he began to study the geographical studies of the ancients: Aristotle, Ptolemy, Strabo and even the Hebrew prophet Ezra to gather some clue as to what lay beyond the ocean sea and to calculate how far across the sea the fabled lands of Cathay and Cipangu, China and Japan, lay. With geographical tracts from the times, he pieces together a theory which places the lands of the Orient much closer to Europe than what most educated

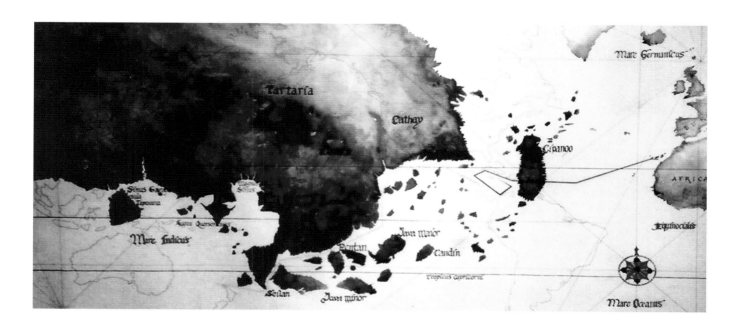

people then believed. Most of the educated men of the time thought the earth a sphere and most believed that, in theory, a ship could reach the East by sailing west, but they also believed that it was too far, in practicality, to accomplish such a feat. They, of course, were more correct in their assumptions than Columbus; but his perseverance in proposing to do something about it and his keen observation as to how to accomplish it were the spark of genius which opened the eyes of the world to the existence of the Americas. No one in Europe or Asia even suspected such a find.

The grand plan was presented to King John II of Portugal in 1484. John was a young, aggressive monarch anxious to hear of any exploits of exploration and discovery, and a 33 year old Columbus had readied his pitch. The Portuguese King had been very encouraging and interested in Columbus's idea but stopped short of a go-ahead. Portugal was more concerned with furthering her voyages down the coast of Africa and an eastern route to the Indies around the African mainland. Five years before this meeting with King John, Columbus had married a young lady of Portuguese nobility and had had a son, Diego. Within a short time after the birth of his son, his wife had unfortunately passed away and he was left grieving, still steadfast in his passionate dreams of the grand enterprise and with the responsibility of taking care of his son. Columbus loved Diego and always looked to his care and education. With King John's lack of decision and with Diego at his side, he goes to Huelva, Spain, a southwestern province on the Portuguese border. His deceased wife had had a sister in Huelva who might help him care for little Diego and he would try to present his grand enterprise to the Spanish crown. While sailing up the *Río Tinto,* the River Tinto, en route to the port of Palos, alongside Huelva, he catches a glimpse of the monastery of *la Rábida,* an institution of Franciscan friars who serve the nearby ports and the seamen who are familiar with explorations into the Atlantic. The friars are also very knowledgeable in the lore of the sea, hospitable to travelers and they

The Monastery of "La Rábida,"
Palos, Spain

often conduct schooling for young boys. There is a romantic vignette of Columbus and his son Diego arriving at the port of Palos and walking along the dusty road which led them to the monastery door of *la Rábida*. There, Columbus asks at the gate for bread and water for his little son and is invited to remain as guests on hearing of his travels from Lisbon. The story continues with his meeting Brother *Antonio de Marchena*, head of the friary and a man of high repute as an astronomer. Highly educated friars, familiar with the sea and dedicated to the service of God; a fortuitous meeting for the man with a vision.

How scintillating must have been the discussions between the thirty-four year old Columbus and the engaging *Fray Antonio*. Against the backdrop of a star-studded Andalusian night, on the upper story of the Brothers' living quarters, in the refectory or in one of the drawing rooms, a passionate young Columbus comes to know the good Friar and expounds on his great enterprise to sail west to the Indies. His words fall on sympathetic, encouraging ears; and through his heartfelt litany of beliefs, Columbus shows himself to be devoted to the Holy Faith and sincerely desirous of bringing more souls into the body of Christ. His zeal and experience convince the good Friar to

The upper rooms and refectory in the Monastery of "La Rábida"

use his connections to introduce Columbus to some of the most powerful men in the kingdom and eventually to the Queen herself. These inspirational interchanges with *Fray Antonio* pushed the young navigator to more study and to prepare himself for the tribunals that would lie before him. One could say that there would be many more dramatic high points in the life of Columbus, but probably none more mellow or more satisfying than these resonant discussions in the monastery of *la Rábida* between himself and the worldly Friar.

Much of the rest is history. A royal commission is brought together at the University of Salamanca and Columbus presents his grand enterprise before them. Great questions remain and no clear cut decision is reached. Politically, the kingdoms of Castile and Aragon are still at war with the kingdom of Granada in the south to gain control of the whole Iberian peninsula in the spirit of nationalism that the monarchs are spearheading. This puts Columbus's grand enterprise on hold, but the developing mutual respect between Columbus and Queen Isabel and his being given a small stipend for his living expenses continue to give him hope of the Spanish monarchs' support. Six more years of waiting, frustration and study until January, 1492, when the forces of Castile and Aragon finally defeat the kingdom of Granada and lay claim to the rest of the peninsula, excepting, of course, the kingdom of Portugal. And within a few months, the Queen and her closest advisors accede to Columbus's demands in a document known as the Capitulations of Santa Fe, Santa Fe being the monarchs' quarters within the precinct of the Alhambra, Granada. Spain needed to follow up her conquest of Granada and to keep pace with the reality of Portuguese exploration and colonization. If Columbus could accomplish what he claimed, this would be a great achievement towards solidifying Spain's remarkable gains of 1492. If not, the cost of the voyage was not so extravagant to negate the possibilities; and so, Columbus makes ready and sets sail from the port of Palos on August 3, 1492, to make history and to forever change the way we would look at the world.

The First Voyage across the ocean sea is the stuff that dreams are made of. Firm in his conviction of a positive outcome and personally devoted to his faith, he plows ahead, virtually alone in his steadfast-

"The Capitulations of Santa Fe," the permission Columbus received from the King and Queen

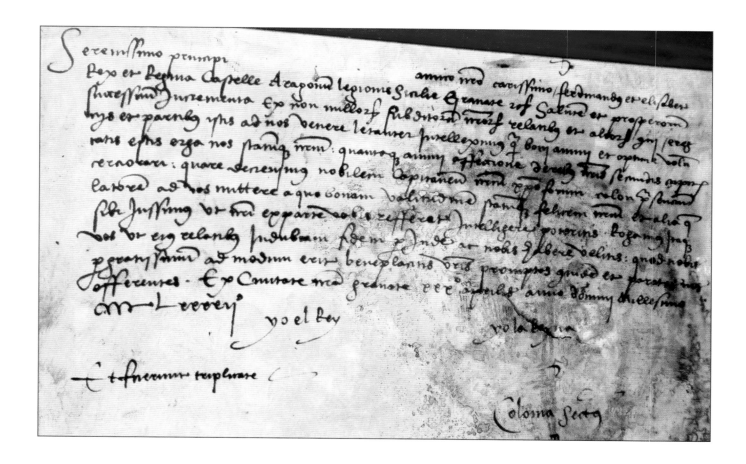

Isolated section of the shoreline in Palos, Spain, where Columbus began his First Voyage

ness, to discover a New World, even though his aim was to reach the Orient. With a crew that comes to the point of mutiny, dwindling stores of food and medicines on board, he stays his course by dead reckoning and prays fervently to the Virgin and her Son for guidance; "*Jesus and Mary be with us along the way.*" The fateful cry of "Land" on October 12, 1492, was met with a spiritual catharsis by the Grand Admiral the likes of which few people in this world will ever experience and since then, history has taken a new turn.

The Santa Maria, Palos, Spain, and the Admiral's quarters below deck

Hardworking, self-educated, responsible, adventurous, highly moral, devoted to his faith, loyal, respectful of others, Columbus was one of those solitary historical figures who lived the dream which had enfolded his life and despite all "the slings and arrows of outrageous fortune," made the most important geographical discovery in modern times. And not only for his great discovery of the Americas, but also, for his navigational skills in successfully crossing an ocean which had never been crossed; his voyages sought to open up the knowledge of oceanic travel for future generations and the development of world trade through the emerging mercantilism of the sixteenth century. The oceans could now be crossed. To be familiar with his life and the times in which he lived will always remain a special fascination to me in realizing what one human can accomplish, even in the face of overwhelming odds.

3. From Isabela to Santo Tomás

IN 1847, THOMAS HENEKEN, an American lawyer living in the Dominican Republic, wrote to Washington Irving telling him that "the route over which Columbus traced his course from Isabela to the mountains of Cibao exists in all its primitive rudeness . . . ; and it is somewhat surprising that, of this first and remarkable footprint of the European in the New World, there does not at the present day exist the least tradition of its former name or importance."

This inland journey undertaken by Columbus was his first and only journey into the interior of any of his discoveries. He was eager to witness firsthand this new land of incredible beauty and to gauge for himself the natives' account of gold within the mountains of the Cibao, the mountainous region in the interior; and because of the Dominican "situation", the land has not changed in the 500 years since he made the journey. In supreme paradox, the land which Columbus had envisioned for such dreamt-of development, lies today as it was seen then. It seemed too good to be true! Here was this fab-

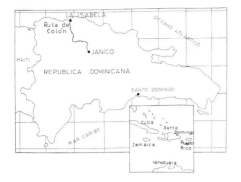

ulous New World as seen through the eyes of the Grand Admiral himself in its "primitive rudeness" without commercial development, without tourism and without urbanization. To cross the rivers he crossed and to see the beautiful vistas he saw, practically in their pristine state, was to telescope 500 years of history and to bear witness to the great phenomenon which was the discovery of the New World. My friend Luis Camilo and I had mounted motorbikes to follow the Admiral's expedition over roads, rocky paths and across rivers to cover in four days what Columbus had covered in four days at the head of a group of 400 men.

The starting point was the site of the first permanent settlement in the New World, Isabela, named by Columbus in honor of his Queen. I, who have always been fond of etymologies and beginnings, was especially keen on exploring the site of Isabela. Here was the beginning of American history as we know it, the beginning of European colonization. Remember, the natives had no written language and lacked any historical records. After discovering this land of captivating beauty on his first voyage in 1492, Columbus had returned to the Spanish Isle in January, 1494, to begin the work of colonization. He

The excavation site of Isabela, the first European colony in the Americas

knew that the land held great promise for development because of its fertility, the gentle manner of the handsome, native population and the reports he had received of mineral wealth in the mountains beyond. When he saw that La Navidad, the fort he had left with 39 men from the first voyage had vanished without a trace, he pushed eastward along the northern coast to find a site which would better serve as a settlement. He probably intended to push ahead to Puerto Plata, the landlocked port seen on the first voyage, but strong headwinds had deterred the fleet so that because of the weariness of the people and the livestock from the long sea voyage, he chose a small headland about twenty miles to the west of Puerto Plata and as expeditiously as possible disembarked his crew of 1,200 men and his livestock cargo to begin the job of colonization. Aside from the crew's weariness, this headland site with its approximately two-acre mesa seemed easily defensible and had a fresh water stream just to the western edge of the mesa and, very importantly, was in a direct line to a path leading into the gold-bearing streams of the Cibao region according to the natives' reports.

Unlike the English in Jamestown who brought a little more than a hundred men in three tiny ships to settle Virginia and exploit her resources under charter from the Virginia Company of London more than 100 years later; the Spanish came with 1,200 men in seventeen ships with seeds to plant, livestock to tend and experts in building, agriculture and mining; and, mostly, at the direct expense of the Crown. For Columbus, Isabela was to be the foundations of a city which would last for all time; but as often occurred in these initial sites of settlement throughout the Americas, like Jamestown, the first sites were later abandoned for more practical vantage points by the colonists who came afterwards. And so, the little town of Isabela, the first European settlement in the New World, found itself on the wane after a dozen years of settlement and became over the centuries, an area of overgrown brush and forgotten significance.

Colonization was an arduous task. Within a week's time, after disembarkation, a third of the crew fell sick, including Columbus himself. Refusal to do any manual labor by the "gentlemen" only sought to aggravate the situation and Columbus struggled against his own physical incapicitance to maintain order and command in the face of his still being considered a foreigner, a Genovese, by a number of these first adventurers in the New World. Yet, even with all the trouble, seeds were planted, scouting parties were sent to reconnoiter the land and the germinal elements of a town were built.

Archeological excavations have uncovered the probable layout of the town with Columbus's quarters and the little church bordering the plaza (the town square) and a warehouse for supplies at the opposite end of the mesa close to an incline which served as an unloading ramp from the beach up to the mesa. The officers' quarters filled in the upper section of the mesa while the rest of the colonists constructed their dwellings in the more inland, lower, section. This contrasts considerably with the film "1492" which premiered in 1992 to commemorate the 500th anniversary of the Discovery of America. The movie which starred Gérard Depardieu as Columbus dramatically portrayed the Admiral's angst in his bid to sail west to the Indies, but the latter half of the film with the construction of Isabela and the

Proposed organization of La Isabela. Note Columbus's house and the tiny church in the left and right corners of the plaza, respectively, and the warehouse in the upper-right corner, all surrounded by a rampart with small sentry boxes

(Map taken from *Como pudo ser la Isabela,* Bottin Castellanos and Dr. Carlos Dobal)

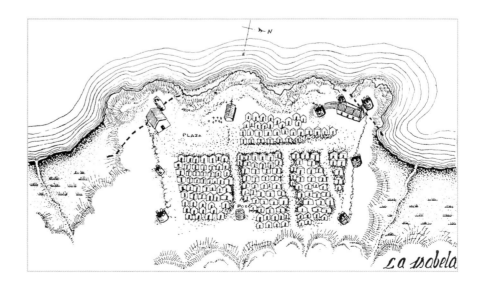

events which followed settlement were mostly fabrication. The film had the Spaniards expending a great effort to raise a bell into a church of grand proportions as if religious frenzy had commanded the colonists' initial efforts at settlement. Nothing could be further from the truth. The actual dimensions of the first Christian temple in the New World measured a modest 15 yards in length by 6 yards in width with a small bell hung from a nearby tree; the first Mass was celebrated just four days after the landing on January 6, the feast of the Epiphany, in what were only the foundations of the church to be. The film had the Spaniards in brutal, outright warfare with the natives and amongst themselves from the outset. This was, also, completely false and a somewhat morose take on the situation at that point; and the wholesale illness which had befallen the colony was not even brought out in the film. A week after landing, three to four hundred men fell ill, a third of their number. The long journey to get to Isabela, the hard work to get things organized, the change in climate from what the crew had been used to and the change in diet based upon the natives' food; all took their toll in the crew's falling ill. The Admiral, himself, had succumbed to the prevalent illness, too; but within six weeks' time, he began to recover his strength, and eagerly planned his journey into the interior at the head of 400 men, on horseback and on foot, to the gold-bearing region of the Cibao.

March 12, 1494, Columbus led his expedition of four days' journey south from Isabela into the Cibao region amid flags unfurled and to the sound of drums and trumpets. With helmets and corselets shining in the tropical sun and with the fearful weapons of the day: arquebuses, lances, swords, etc., the 400 rode out in military file to manifestly display the pomp and might of Spain to all the natives who might see or be in earshot. The purpose of this majestic expedition was to construct a fortress in the Cibao region which would oversee the work of the mines and to maintain the peace with the native tribes.

Luis mounted up for the ride

As mentioned above, my friend Luis and I had mounted our motorbikes to follow Columbus's journey in March, 1994, five hundred years to the date that the Grand Admiral himself had led *his* expedition. We spent the first night in a small *casa de campesino,* a peasant hut, on a straw mattress upon this hallowed ground within the lower portion of the Isabela mesa to bear witness to the whirr of the wind and the breaking of the waves along the beach as the only sounds heard within the night's quiet and then set off south the next morning along a sandy ridge covered in buckthorns to reach the point on the Bajabonico River where the Grand Admiral had crossed with his men five hundred years before. This crossing is less than a mile from Isabela. For much of the year the Bajabonico is at very low tide, but in the spring, the river swells because of the seasonal rains. Curiously, the name *Bajabonico,* the softer sounding version in the Aragonese dialect instead of the Castilian, *bonito,* reminded me of the driving force in the Discovery of the New World was, in great part, a result of the union of the Kingdoms of *Castilla* and *Aragón* under Fernando and Isabel.

With no bridges, very few buildings and no signposts, Luis and I began our journey of not only historical fascination, but one of ineffable beauty which is really a tantalizing introduction into the physiognomy of this land.

Crossing the Bajabonico

At the Bajabonico, we had to enlist the services of three of the native boys to help carry our bikes across the river. Even at swollen conditions the river could easily be forded on foot, but the transport of our iron steeds needed the carriers' help. As already mentioned, this was exactly the place the Grand Admiral had crossed with his expeditionary force five hundred years before. We were off on our authentic trail of history.

A short distance beyond we crossed the *Unijica* Rivulet which was essentially dry even with the swollen state of the Bajabonico and found ourselves on a dry, rocky road leading into the great Northern Range, the *Cordillera Septentrional*. Even from the settlement of Isabela, the mountains can be seen in the distance, about ten miles away. The

The coastal plain with the Northern Range in the background

61

The incredible beauty, as seen from the mountain pass

rocks in the sandy roadway, big enough to topple a bike but small enough to lend substance to the road itself, cut through a wide swath of coastal plain where the locals cultivate small produce. Coastal plains are generally fertile because of the surrounding bodies of water, but this plain was sandier and less fertile than most. The aridness is probably due to the paucity of river water and to the fact that even though the mesa upon which Isabela sits is right on the ocean, it faces due west and is passed over by the northwesterly trade winds along the shore. These are the winds which bring the accompanying rains in their season. It is not a long trek to reach the foot of the mountains where the dramatic contrast of greener, more lush vegetation within the mountain fastness is an incredible sight to behold.

With the ascent into the mountains, a land of fabled beauty comes into full view; thick, luxuriant vegetation with an almost other-worldly quality to it. Streams running in all directions, palm trees growing on the mountain-tops, banana trees interspersed with mahogany and ebony to the point that the Spaniards must have been overwhelmed to see such an earthly paradise before them. Columbus had sent a group of *hidalgos,* gentlemen, ahead to clear and widen a native path through this mountain fastness so that his expedition could press forward with safety and order. To this day the pass is called the *Puerto de los Hidalgos,* the Gentlemen's Pass, in honor of the noblemen who first cleared it. The Spanish word *hidalgo (hijo de algo),* "son of something," generally referred to the younger sons of Spanish noblemen, who retained very little but a title because of the Spanish custom of primogeniture whereby the eldest son received the lion's share of his father's estate. This is why so many of the first noblemen to come to the New World were these *hidalgos* who sought their fame and fortune far away from their native soil. The Pass, which aligns itself with the modern road, suddenly takes a zag to the east through a split in the range and passes a glen surrounded by great, royal palms and mahogany trees. From here, the first glimpse of the wondrous *Vega Real,* the Royal Plain, comes into view.

The Royal Plain which lies between the Northern and the Central ranges, also known as the *Cibao* range, is one of the most wondrous places in the world, especially when seen from the *Puerto de los Hidalgos*. When Columbus saw it, he looked at it with awe and gave great thanks to God for its beauty and its astonishing fertility. A valley of rich, black soil which nurtures vegetation everywhere, it stands in dramatic contrast to the relatively arid coastal plain already traversed. Here, in the *Vega Real,* banana trees form borders to fertile meadows and waterways seem ubiquitous. Royal palms frame fields of crops and all the harmonious elements seem to caress the wanderer in his passage through her heartland. Luis and I descended the declivity from the *Puerto de los Hidalgos* to follow the road down to the Crossing of the Guaiacs, *el Cruce de los Guayacanes,* from the Taíno word, *guayacán. Guayacán* has come down to us as the "tree of life," *lignum vitae,* because of the stimulant effect of its wood.

At the crossing, the road proceeds either east or west to parallel the substantial river called the *Yaque del Norte* which lies a few miles south of the crossing. The *Yaque* has its origin deep in the *Cordillera Central,* the Central Range, and follows a flare-like path to skirt the cities of La Vega and Santiago de los Caballeros on its trajectory north, and then west, to empty into the Atlantic at Monte Cristi. Columbus called this river the River of Reeds, unaware that it was the same one he had seen on his first voyage at Monte Cristi and had previously called the River of Gold. Luis and I proceeded east towards Santiago and passed the turnoff to the small town of *Maimón* with its river of the same name. *Maimón* is a name of Arab origin and reminded me of the great twelfth century Jewish physician and philosopher from Spain whose name was Maimonides. This was a way in which the Arabs came to name people, by taking the father's first name and adding *es* or *ez* as a suffix to mean "son of"; which is why today, so many Spanish surnames end in *ez* or *es: Rodríguez,* son of Rodrigo; *Pérez,* son of Pedro; *Domínguez,* son of Domingo, etc. . . . *Maimónides,* son of Maimón.

Along the main road through this lush valley in which one almost expects the Jolly Green Giant to appear at any moment, Luis and I opted for secondary and tertiary roads that brought us closer to the northern edge of the *Yaque del Norte* to come upon the spot that the Spaniards crossed five hundred years before. The expedition crossed at a point called, appropriately enough, *Pontón.* Those on horseback crossed without a problem while the foot soldiers were ferried across this River of Reeds, that is, the *Yaque del Norte,* in special watercrafts which the natives called *canoas,* canoes. Unlike the film version of 1492, Columbus made sure that the natives' property and dignity were respected by the Spaniards and there was a general feeling of goodwill amongst them all. The Spaniards were so intoxicated with the natural beauty of the *Vega Real* and the prospects of finding gold in the mountain streams beyond that there really was no cause for friction at this point.

Through this valley of incredible fertility the expedition pressed on towards the Central Mountain chain. Within a short distance the land becomes more rolling with small patches of denuded mounds surrounded by verdant areas of royal palms. It as if Nature herself had created a special patchwork quilt with this unique design to lure the traveler further into her heart. We have now come upon the southern flank of the famous Cibao region of the Republic. And, finally, we

The fabled Cibao region

65

arrived at our goal, the small village of *Jánico,* with its river of the same name, on the northern side of the Central Range. A few miles outside the town is a bend in the river which surrounds a natural headland on which the Spaniards had built a small wooden fort in order to coordinate their mining efforts and to maintain the peace amongst the natives. The fort was named *Santo Tomás* by Columbus for the disbeliever who might doubt the finding of gold in these mountain streams and the ineffable fertility and beauty of the land. The

The bluff upon which the Spaniards built Fort Santo Tomás. The commemorative plaque was placed in 1594, as the 100th anniversary celebration of its founding.

terrain remains today much as it was experienced back then; no souvenir stands, no welcome center, no commercial exploitation to detract from the sanctity of the place; just the headland, or mesa, similar to the one at Isabela, surrounded by a crystal pure stream shaded by thick vegetation of a more mountainous variety. I, who tend to avoid drinking from any river in this day and age, had actually drunk from the *Jánico* because of its obvious lack of contamination and a certain feeling of invitation from the water's crystal clear appearance. The stream dances over shiny pebbles interspersed with colored stones that were made even more lustrous by the glistening waters flowing across them.

It is truly uncanny how this trail has remained, almost in its pristine state, after five centuries' time; but, it is a special delight to be able to experience almost exactly what the Grand Admiral had experienced in this first chapter in the history of the New World.

CIVITAS S. DOMINICI
in Hispaniola

A Templum primarium
B Forum
C Castellum
D Hortus Communis
E Cœnobium S. Barbara

4. Santo Domingo, the First City of the Americas

Ningún pueblo de España, ni Barcelona, le hacía ventaja en cuanto a edificios.

—Oviedo, 16th century

No city in Spain, not even Barcelona, was more favored in her buildings.

Throughout the 16th century Santo Domingo reigned as the most famous city of the western world. As the political and economic center for Spain's great adventure in the Americas, Santo Domingo became the "key, the gateway and the starting point" for all the efforts of the mother country in the newly discovered lands. All shipping both to and from the New World had to clear customs here; the seat of governmental authority in the name of the viceroy was established here; and judicial decisions affecting all of the newly discovered lands were handed down through the tribunals in the *Casas Reales,* the Royal Houses. Spain's assertion of authority dictated that she build a city which would uphold the dignity of this authority.

"Santo Domingo de la isla Isabela," from a 1502 frontispiece of a book on Marco Polo's exploits in the Orient. Most people still believed that the Spanish Isle was within the Orient.

To further the quest towards colonization, exploration, the working of the mines, the pacification and Christianization of the natives and the development of some new form of agriculture, a monumental effort had to be launched. For such a commitment thousands of miles away from the mother country, builders and artisans of every kind were sent; experts in mining and agriculture, soldiers to further the conquest and pacification of the natives, notaries to record real estate transactions and draw up business contracts; lawyers, doctors; and, of course, the clergy to bring the natives into the knowledge of Christ and to give spiritual guidance to the colonists. Along with these professionals came others who sought adventure, wealth and an easy life. From the time of Columbus's second voyage the Spaniards brought livestock, plants, foodstuffs and all manner of tools to sustain themselves in this new earthly paradise.

For the traveler, Santo Domingo stands as a unique, awe-inspiring experience. With the weighty investment in men and matériel during the opening years of the 16th century, this monumental effort by the newcomers produced a magnificent European city which reflected late medieval and early Renaissance architecture and has no equal in the western hemisphere. It was never to be duplicated in the rest of the Americas; for by the time the great new cities of Mexico, Peru, Venezuela, Colombia and the neighboring Antilles came into being; the ornate architectural styles prevalent in Europe at the time, the Baroque and the Rococo, had pretty much replaced 16th century Renaissance forms, so that what we think of today as "colonial" architecture in Spanish America is usually with a picture of one of the great urban Baroque cathedrals on the mainland or of one of the humble mission styles of the southwestern U.S. UNESCO has declared the colonial zone of Santo Domingo a world cultural heritage for its unique and historical character.

Santo Domingo was the first city of the western world and it is here that American history began. The *Taíno* Indians on the island

Gothic portal in the old wall of the city

had lacked a written language so that their tradition had been an oral one. That is not to say that their culture had been in any way impoverished, and from the beginning, efforts were made, especially among the Franciscan and Dominican friars, to study the customs and the language of the Natives together with a study of the natural flora and fauna of the island.

In 1502, Fernando and Isabel, their Catholic Majesties, sent a new governor to the island by the name of *Nicolás de Ovando*. The knight of a military order, a man of steadfast purpose with strict devotion to the rule of law, Ovando becomes the catalyst who lays out the new city in a grid, distributes housing sites and begins the construction of houses of stone to mark the permanence and authority of the colony. He was one of those unsung heroes who dealt with the arrogant and lawless reality of the adventurers, the natives who were still in rebellion and the demands necessary to further the survival and perma-

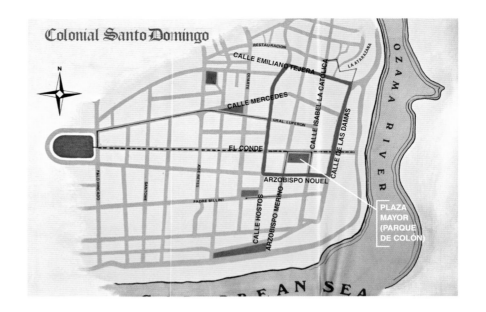

Colonial Santo Domingo

nence of the colony. By the time of his departure in 1509, the city had taken on the beginnings of its special character. He had overseen the construction of roads, houses of worship, buildings for schools, councils, convents, hospitals and the jails; and he had launched a system of internal taxation to insure the gains he had begun under his administration. By 1509, the city had taken on its rectangular shape within the limits of the modern-day streets of *Emiliano Tejera* in the north to *Arzobispo Nouel* in the south, the *Calle de las Damas* in the east to the *Calle Hostos* in the west together with an epicenter as the *Plaza Mayor,* or the modern-day *Parque de Colón.* Some of these stone structures sit upon the same sites as they did from the beginning.

Aside from its aesthetic and functional aspects, architecture has always had its political considerations. Creating a well ordered town with fine, handsome structures of stone conferred an image of prestige, authority and permanence so that Santo Domingo became a statement of Spain's thrust into the New World. Buildings of hewn stone with architectural graces of the age made this statement a reality.

The first stone structure known as the *Casa del Cordón,* the House of the Cord, was built in 1503 by Francisco Garay. Garay had come to *Española* with Columbus as a notary and had made a fortune in the

La Casa del Cordón

gold mines. He built this distinctive house to maintain a noble presence in the place he came to call his home. The entranceway is framed by a magnificent cord of stone which was symbolic of the Order of the Franciscans, the famous cord of St. Francis; which, by the way, was Garay's namesake as well. A substantial edifice with Romanesque perspectives in respect to its heaviness and its fortress-like character, yet decidedly Renaissance in the perfect symmetry of detail and its flattened archway bordered by a band of elegant vegetation worked in stone. This fine detail in stone belonged to an early sub-style of the Renaissance called the Plateresque, "silver-like," for it compared to the fine detail of the silversmiths working the metal to create elegant and intricate filigrees, as in the refined Damascene silverwork of the Muslim artisans of Toledo. Within this Plateresque framework are a series of stone pearls which were a late Spanish Gothic variation within the so-called Isabelina style, the style in vogue during the latter part of Queen Isabel's reign, roughly 1480–1505. The Isabelina style, which was a florid expression of the Gothic, included exquisite stone traceries within the windows of the pointed arches and ele-

The House of the Constables of Castile, Burgos, Spain. Their Catholic Majesties received Columbus from the return of his second voyage to the New World, here, in this house. Note the Franciscan cord above the door as an architectural antecedent to the House of the Cord in Santo Domingo.

73

ments of a more exotic origin, like Moorish and Byzantine accents. The pearls may have been, specifically, of Byzantine influence and are ubiquitous in the Isabelina style. The entire building reflects the simplicity and the sobriety of the Spanish Renaissance and is a unique, visual experience. As the first stone building of the New World, it commands a special air of distinction and majesty, which was probably Garay's intention; but its existence, here, on a street in the old town seems almost surreal in the vision of such a striking medieval-Renaissance edifice that seems almost out of place in the Western hemisphere. This same, surreal sensation of unique character is reflected in so many of the buildings of Santo Domingo.

Probably the most medieval looking structure of the city, taken in its totality, is the *Casa del Tostado*. Built some twenty years after the *Casa del Cordón* by the notary Francisco Tostado, who came with *Nicolás de Ovando* in 1502, the house makes a clear statement of the Isabelina style of the late Gothic period. Similar to the elegant palaces of the nobility in the late 15th and early 16th centuries, the twin win-

The House of Tostado
(Casa del Tostado)

74

dows above the doorway give an especially graceful appearance to an otherwise simple entranceway. The elegant stone traceries within the windows display more of a decorative than a functional support along with another row of pearls below the stone bracket, both strongly characteristic of the Isabelina style. These buildings relate intimately to the ground on which they sit and both offer an engaging, Old World look to the passerby.

The most dramatic structure in the old city and the one which most identifies with Santo Domingo is, without question, the *alcázar de don Diego Colón,* the fortress-palace of Diego Columbus. Built in 1510 by the new governor of *Española* and the son of the Grand Admiral himself, the *alcázar* is, also, an elegant Renaissance building reminiscent of Spanish and Italian noble palaces of the late 15th and early 16th centuries. Two main bodies at the extremes joined by an airy transept of double galleries on two levels, the *alcázar* stands as a sumptuous contrast between Renaissance architectural refinement and a backdrop of tropical luxuriance. As seen from the heights of the neighboring *Casas Reales,* the scene could almost be likened to the fabled Hanging Gardens of Nebuchadnezzar as pictured in some of the old

The palace-fortress of Diego Columbus

Left: The "alcázar" as seen from the "Casas Reales" (the Royal Houses)

Right: An early lithograph titled "House of Don Diego Columbus"

romantic lithographs. The lower level gallery displays tall, rounded arches with subtle double recesses framing the arch and simple Doric capitals as the supports; the upper level gallery displays a more flattened arch with similar recesses, Doric capitals and a delicate Gothic balustrade giving an especially diaphanous quality to the facade as a whole. The interior is beautifully complemented with a display of furnishings from the period and proudly impresses with the elegance and moderation of Spanish décor.

On passing into the entranceway at the center of the transept, the reception room is seen with a variety of antiquities including an armored steed and his rider. Somehow, this does not detract from the reality of the décor. The piece which draws my attention most, however, is a crucified Christ over the left archway, which is probably the oldest piece in the *alcázar* and is, in fact, an early 14th century Gothic sculpture of wood. Gothic sculpture, which was usually elongated, served mainly as a decorative artifice to Gothic architecture in general, without human expressiveness. The Romanesque sculpture which preceded it told a story and the Renaissance sculpture which

followed gave testament to the intensity of human emotions in its facial features, but the Gothic remained between the other two great periods with a look of impassiveness. Here, an elongated, impassive Christ appears resigned and without any expression as he suffers through his Passion. Passing into the south wing which contains the kitchen area, there hangs a *retablo,* that is a sculpture in relief, which is probably from the mid 15th century and displays a whole scenario of that day on Calvary with poignant facial expressions in all its characters. To the left side of this beautiful piece is a characterization of the Three Marys at the Crucifixion, brokenhearted, reflective and sad, easily perceived in their faces. The walk across the two rooms bridges a time-span of 150 years in the styles of sculpture, from Gothic to Renaissance.

At the rear of the right wing, that is, the side facing the river, there is a stone circular stairway that seems to conjure up images of medieval castles and secret passageways. It leads to the second floor gallery with its expansive view of the River Ozama and an especially clear view through the upper transept. The central doorway into the tran-

A sculpture in relief (un retablo)

77

sept reveals a rounded arch with a delicate arabesque ornamentation and a majestic *reja,* ornamental ironwork. The passageway into the northern wing is all in brick, which was a notable Arab contribution to building construction in the Iberian Peninsula. The Arabs were among the best builders in the world and they left their stamp everywhere in medieval Spain.

The bedrooms follow with the first being that of *doña María de Toledo,* wife to Diego Columbus. The forms of address, *don* for a man

and *doña* for a lady, placed before a first name connote respect even when using the given name. Spanish is more flexible in this usage and English has no equivalent. The bed is a four-posted Renaissance rendition of probable late 16th or early 17th century with rich wooden turnings highlighted with gilded ornamentation. The cornice clearly displays an intricacy which was characteristic of the Mannerist style, a style that originated in late 16th century Italy and intended to give ornamentation to the otherwise stark Renaissance forms. Mannerism made use of allegorical heads, Cupids, acanthus leaves and vines in intricate stone or wood carvings while maintaining the basic look of the Renaissance. The protruding, gilded flecks in the turnings go along with this style and create an elegant touch without detracting from its classic look. On the wall at the foot of the bed is a delightful closet with the look of a "*confesionario,*" that is, of a church confessional; a refined wooden piece of latticework which blends harmoniously into its interior.

On crossing into *don Diego*'s bedroom, there is a small anteroom which was probably used as a study. Here, as in some of the other rooms, there is a special note given to the small stone seats facing each other and set into the window space. The viceroys would take com-

fort in a place to moderate the tropical heat and enjoy a welcome breeze while able to contemplate what was going on in the world outside. And the seats are covered with velvet cushions, which probably lent a softness and a royalty to these stately perches. The bedroom itself is simple in its proportions and its furnishings. One thing *don Diego* was sure to have was a clear view of the *Casas Reales,* the Royal Houses, and the first street of the town, *la Calle de las Damas,* the Street of the Courtiers (female), for it was here, that legend has it, that *doña María* would walk with her ladies-in-waiting during the evening *paseo,* the nightly stroll.

At the head of *la Calle de las Damas* is the stately edifice of the *Casas Reales,* the Royal Houses. This handsome building is really two buildings; the larger one on the right is constructed of hewn stone and has an early Plateresque/Renaissance doorway which served as the residence for the Governors of the island; while the one on the left faced with brick and *mampostería,* rubble-work, housed the Royal Courts, the Royal Accounting office and the Chancellery, which was the diplomatic liaison for the colony. I have always been intrigued with this technique of rubble-work (*mampostería*), the taking of

Las Casas Reales (The Royal Houses)

rough stones and positioning them into a mortar mixture within a wooden frame to hold it together until dry. When dry, it is as hard as if it were solid rock. It is amazing to contemplate how much of this rubble-work has lasted for the past five hundred years despite the elements, the hurricanes and the earthquakes. Although the building today houses a museum containing artifacts from the three centuries of the colonial period; to me, it is the building itself which is so striking. Austere, imposing, it seems to exude all the authority it was meant to convey, whether from the facade or from the inner patios with their colonnaded galleries.

Heading down *la Calle de las Damas,* the oldest street in the New World, past the noble residences of the family *Dávila,* past the *Ovando* portal and past the living quarters of *Hernán Cortés* where he lived for years before striking out to make history in the conquest of Mexico; the sojourner makes his/her way through to the *Calle del Conde* until arriving at the cathedral.

The first cathedral of the New World is usually approached from the central square, *el Parque de Colón.* The rather unprepossessing facade which faces the park appears as some kind of Neoclassical viewing stand which offered dignitaries a bird's eye view of

La Calle de las Damas (The Street of the Courtiers, female)

the events going on in the *Plaza Mayor* rather than the entrance to a grand monument. But, once inside, the experience becomes magnificent.

La Catedral de Nuestra Señora de la Encarnación, the Cathedral of Our Lady of the Incarnation, was built about the same time as the last great Gothic cathedral in Segovia, Spain, around 1525. It is classically Gothic with its pointed arches and high-flying vaults together with its characteristic tracings to support those vaults; while on the exterior, there are flying buttresses to help support the weight of the heightened walls. Three naves, all about the same height, supported by well-

Above: An alms box in the Cathedral
Right: The Cathedral's vaulting

proportioned columns, collared by a ring of pearls in the *Isabelina* style are as light and airy as I have seen in any cathedral. The subtle progression of the Gothic bands (tracings) from above the collared rings on the columns and into the vaultings above impart an almost "palm-tree" effect to the light-colored stone so that there is a feeling that you are in the midst of a tropical forest instead of in the interior of a great religious monument. Also, the similar heights of the three

naves give the sanctuary the look of a salon rather than some secluded refuge so that light streaming in through the doors and windows from the tropical sun provide an expansive, airy feeling which I have never felt in any other cathedral. The brightness, the openness and the veritable simplicity of this magnificent edifice accord a certain harmony of the cathedral to its tropical surroundings so that there is a resonant feeling of being there without the hustle and the noise of the capital itself. This openness is also evident through the truncated transept, or the lack of a transept, with its doors open on either side so that the visitor can easily see through the great cathedral from the *Parque de Colón,* the main square, to the *Plazoleta de los Curas,* the little Plaza of the Priests; that is, clear through from the north to the south porticos.

The arabesque touches here and there are reminiscent of the contribution Spanish builders of Moorish descent played in the construction of this temple, as well as in the rest of the buildings of the city. One particularly stunning detail is the horseshoe arch in the central

Above: "Alexander Geraldini, citizen of Santo Domingo, a Roman (Catholic) city." Geraldini, the first archbishop of Santo Domingo, initiated the construction of the Cathedral in 1521.

Below: Arabesque tilework

window of the apse. Aside from the cathedrals in Spain which were obvious conversions from earlier mosques, I have never seen such a detail in a Christian sanctuary. The rich wainscoting of the tilework in some of the chapels, especially the first one on the right of the High Altar, also gives note to Spain's Moorish roots. This glazed, blue coloring was the original color of the Spanish tiles, *azulejos,* from the Spanish word, *azul,* meaning "blue," and was a notable Arab contribution to the architecture of medieval Spain.

One of my favorite little buildings in the colonial sector is the *Colegio de Gorjón,* College of *Gorjón. Hernando de Gorjón* was one of the men who arrived with Governor *Ovando* in 1502. He amassed a

Looking through the Cathedral from the south portico to the "Parque de Colón ," the main square

The ramparts surrounding the Cathedral portico

great deal of wealth from his involvement with sugar mills, and being childless, decided to found a college for the study of the sciences and built this school in the mid 1530's for that purpose. A massive Renaissance gateway of hewn stone juts right onto the roadway and is remarkable for its antiquity and simplicity. Before the Haitian occupation of the early 19th century, the upper encasements would have included the shields of *Gorjón*, Emperor Charles V and the city itself. The Haitians, caught up in their own independence and the spillover from the French Revolution, attempted to remove any visible vestige of the nobility. I like to imagine the school as it was when newly founded, with its classrooms facing the sea and sitting atop an incline which is about a half a block from the sea: tropical luxuriance, the refreshing breezes from the sea and eager students in a new school and a New World.

Two of the most romantic architectural finds in the capital lie just to the west of the city on the banks of the *Jaina* (pronounced Hina) River, and most Dominicans do not even know of their existence. They are two sugar mills built in the early 16th century. During the first quarter century, mining for precious metals was the

The sugar mill at Engombe

colony's main source of revenue, but as the quantities of gold extracted had diminished, sugar took its place as the main export during the next quarter century. Columbus had introduced the sugar cane from the Canary Islands on his second voyage, because he believed that it would thrive in this new tropical paradise; and thrive it did. The cane fields seemed to be any and everywhere they might flourish. Here, the cane was grown upstream and thrown into the river to be collected and processed at these two mills. The one nearer to the mouth of the river is called the *Ingenio de Engombe,* the Mill at *Engombe,* and is really a complex of buildings which is enveloped by tropical vegetation today. Coming onto these early 16th century structures in their natural setting, and with usually no one around, is a fabulous experience; the visitor may get the feeling that he/she is rediscovering a piece of history for him/herself that has lain concealed for hundreds of years and the juxtaposition of tropical luxuriance with these early 16th century structures in nothing short of a stunning experience. The first building to appear in view from the dense growth is the two-storied Renaissance palace which served as the administration and accounting nucleus as well as living quarters for

the owners and, maybe, some room as a storehouse. Open, elegant, with all the symmetry and simplicity of the Renaissance, the facade boasts double archways in a semi-elliptical shape on both levels to form the porticos. The basic layout is of two central rooms on each level with four smaller rooms flanking them. Again, we see the little stone seats facing each other and set into the window encasements as in the *alcázar* of Columbus, noble vantage points to watch the work going on, or, just to catch the breeze from the river. It is curious, however, that the windows do not display the same type of symmetry as most Renaissance buildings did at the time; either there was a conscious effort to adapt the building to the business at hand, or there was a tendency to break with pure architectural style, as we see later in the century when the Mannerist sub-style tended to offset some of the obvious symmetry of the classics.

There is a small chapel just to the left of the palace as seen from the approach to the area; small enough to remind anyone familiar with the little Romanesque churches in the north of Spain, yet decidedly of a Renaissance style. The approach brings one face to face with the polygonal apse and a small bell tower which also serves as an abutment to the building. A cupola in the shape of a half-orange and a two-sloped roof complete the picture of quaint solitude for a religious sanctuary that appears to have withdrawn from the worldliness

in which other churches find themselves enmeshed today. And even though the interior has not seen a religious service, maybe for hundreds of years; there is a pleasing serenity to the place and a worthwhile architectural experience to be had, albeit with all the hand-carved graffiti, as opposed to the spray-can variety, seen throughout. A small room which served as a sacristy juts out from the right of the main altar and a small niche which probably contained the image of one of the saints is seen between the altar and the entrance to the sacristy.

Further up the incline and several meters from the chapel is a rectangular building which may have served as a warehouse or as slave quarters. Within the first decade of the 16th century, the native population began to wane, in large part because of the lack of immunity to European diseases, and the Spaniards began to import African blacks to bear the labor-intensive work of the mines and the cane fields. The name *Engombe* is one of the few African place names to have survived the centuries and refers to a Bantu tribe from the upper part of the Congo. Towards 1550, however, the importation of slaves was no longer permitted in the colony, and within the years that followed, the extreme subsistence conditions of the Spanish Isle were partially responsible for bringing about a larger measure of social equality among the races.

Halfway between the palace and the river are the ruins of the mill itself. A large, circular grindstone outlined by a small stone barrier mark the site where a mule would have pulled the upper stone to extract the sugar from the cane. To visit this isolated sugar mill in its natural surroundings is to gain a feeling for the beginnings of American history in all its poignant realities.

A few miles up the river is another sugar mill which appears in none of the guide books and, even, very few of the history books. *Palavé* is a solitary edifice in the Renaissance style with a much different look from *Engombe*. It was built at about the same time, but there

Palavé

is precious little documentation relating to its history. It may very well be the oldest, unrestored building on the island and sits handsomely among the tall grasses which surround it. The traveler can find it by consulting a good map of the Santo Domingo area and locating the village of *Manoguayabo* which borders the northwest section of the city, just before the connection to the Duarte Highway, north. As for locating *Engombe,* it is much more difficult to find and requires a knowledgeable person in the colonial sector together with a trustworthy cab driver who can understand his directions. None of the cab drivers and none of the concierges in the hotels is familiar with its location, but for the more adventurous; by taking the main highway west towards *San Cristóbal,* the explorer can make the last turn-off to the right onto a dirt road just a hundred meters before the toll booth which will lead to *Engombe.* Both *Engombe* and *Palavé* are well worth the effort.

In the eastern part of the island, between the resorts of *Casa de Campo,* in *la Romana,* and *Punta Cana,* lies the small village of *San Rafael de Yuma.* Even though this is far afield from Santo Domingo, there stands an architectural sight which is nothing short of surreal. Here, in the middle of a sugar cane field which seems to go on forever, is the fortress-home of *Ponce de León.* A late medieval-Renaissance structure of exceptional robustness, this mansion was built in 1505, and has absolutely nothing to do with its surroundings. Built as an extension of Spanish authority in this heretofore untamed part of the country, the house served as living quarters for the governor of the *Higüey Province, Ponce de León,* and as a refuge in times of native unrest for the colonists who lived nearby. A massive portal of hewn stone is the only opening on the first floor, which gives the building a decidedly medieval look, and there are few windows on the upper level. The massive walls are of *mampostería,* rubble-work, and ingeniously, the walls of the upper story curve outward so that a ladder placed against the side of the building could easily be forced back by

The fortress-palace of Ponce de León, eastern provinces

a push from above. The interior, although restored, is remarkable for its heavy use of wood for the floors and the ceiling and of brick for the central columns helping to support the four sloped roof. Both these elements, wood and brick, were introduced into the Iberian Peninsula by the Moorish builders of the Middle Ages; and, consequently, their use helps to define how Spanish architecture differs, in part, from the architecture of other European countries.

Coming to know these buildings is, in great measure, a coming to appreciate the beginnings of American history and a unique architectural experience, only to be savored here, in the Dominican Republic.

5. Sosúa

THE 1930S AND 40S were hard times for most people in the world: economic depression, a world war and gross atrocities committed against groups of people in the human family for no other reason than their belonging to a particular ethnic group. Many times when coming across some historical event of the time, I tend to think of what was occurring contemporaneously in the world with almost a fixation on the above events. How could people carry on with their lives in the face of such "bad times?" How could there be any cause for merriment or celebration with such a backdrop of depression and war? And, yet, just as the world's problems were coming to a head; the human spirit strove to overcome the evil with art forms which gave us hope: movie musicals, big band sounds, radio, fashion, art deco—they all brought our hearts into a fantasy era which gave us pause from the horrible reality surrounding the times, or in the case of radio, they connected us to the some of the reality.

1938 proved to be a watershed year in the arena of world politics. In March of that year, the German Chancellor, Adolf Hitler, launched

"Rum and Coca-Cola" and the lure of the tropics

(Courtesy of the Coca-Cola Company)

his international play for world power with the *Anschluss,* the annexation of Austria into the Third Reich. Without so much as firing a shot, he bullied the Austrian Chancellor and the Austrian power structure so that he was able to gain complete political dominance within a few weeks' time. Austria had become a part of Germany, and with the annexation came a doubling of the Jewish population under Nazi control, those who found themselves within Germany and, now, the Austrian Jews within the expanded Reich. To bring the plight of Jewish refugees onto the world stage, Franklin D. Roosevelt, the American President, proposed a conference to be held in *Évian-les-Bains,* the famous source for water on the French-Swiss border, which brought together representatives of 32 countries in the free world to attempt to find a safe haven for refugees being persecuted by the Nazis. The Evian Conference in July, 1938, commanded the whole world's attention. Politically, the United States could not absorb any more refugees and the Nazis saw themselves as benefitting from whatever the outcome should be; if other countries would accept Jewish refugees, they would be less problematic for the Reich, and if not, Hitler would state to the world how hypocritical the world's governments were by expressing sympathy for the Jews and doing little or nothing to help them.

Only one government of all the 32 countries at the Conference stood up to offer asylum to those Jews imprisoned within the Reich. Only one country from among the vast expanses of the world's land spaces. The country, the Dominican Republic. President Trujillo of the Dominican Republic offered 100,000 visas and resettlement land on the north shore of this island paradise to those refugees willing to populate and work the land; and this was by no means, any small gesture. Aside from the willingness to make the offer, it took a certain amount of courage and swagger on the part of the Dominican President as it also snubbed the German Chancellor, an action which no other government on earth was willing to do in 1938.

Left: Evian, France, with Lake Geneva and Lausanne, Switzerland, in the background

Some say it was a "backroom" deal between Roosevelt and Trujillo. Some say that Trujillo wanted to form a nucleus of economic productivity in a, then, isolated area of his country. Some say that he just wanted to "whiten" the Dominican population on the north shore to make an even greater contrast from the "blacks" of neighboring Haiti. Whatever motivated him to do so, he saved thousands of Jewish lives from the Holocaust with the Dominican offer rendered at the Evian Conference.

Rafael Leónidas Trujillo Molina, generally referred to as *el tirano* (the tyrant) by his countrymen of today, was a man of his time. A strong man with an uncanny ability for politics and an insatiable appetite for power, he was "elected" President of the Republic in 1930, a year in which the harsh reality of depression was beginning to take hold and people were looking for leaders to lead them out of the hard times. He was born one of eleven children in the quaint little town of *San Cristóbal* just to the west of the capital in 1891. His father, don Pepe, a small businessman who sold construction materials and his mother, a middle class woman of the time. Don Pepe was a likable sort who was well connected in politics, which was an absolute necessity for anyone with position or property during those times. Little Rafael seemed to be more serious and less rowdy than his brothers,

Rafael Leónidas Trujillo Molina

and always concerned himself with having a neat appearance. And, yet, he was a real boy in his love of sports and in his developing an above average interest in the opposite sex during adolescence. At the age of 16, he was capable enough to be hired as a telegraph operator, a government position which required some political pull; and he associated himself with a group of young men interested in politics who aided small time politicians in obtaining contributions from rural general stores with the use of strong-arm tactics.

Shortly thereafter, Trujillo managed to get a permanent job at a sugar plantation as a weigher, a job which required great responsibility, and from there, he was groomed as the chief of a private guard force at the *Andrés* sugar mill at *Boca Chica.* This last position was probably because of his familiarity with strong-arm tactics and here he honed his skills by settling disputes, breaking up fights, as well as arresting criminals at the point of a gun. He learned how to make a culprit an informer, to use diplomacy whenever he could and he even took to taking bribes on occasion. It was a tough job, but one which was preparing him for his future career as the strong man of the Republic.

In 1916, when Trujillo was 25 years old, the United States found it necessary to send an invasionary force of marines to occupy the Republic. This action, illegal as it may have been, had the purpose of bringing about some kind of order to a government which had fallen into complete chaos. Custom duties were being diverted and the government had become ineffectual. War had broken out in Europe and it was only a matter of time before the United States would become involved. Germany had eyed with interest *Samaná* Bay on the northeastern coast of the Republic as a base to disrupt shipping lanes to and from the Panama Canal and President Wilson reluctantly formalized the decision to invade. The U.S. military had established a National Guard within the Republic to replace military control of the civilian population and Trujillo came highly recommended for officers' candidate training. He gained a commission as Second Lieutenant and shortly thereafter entered a Military Academy established under the auspices of U.S. advisors from which he became a Captain. He was subsequently singled out with qualities which marked him for yet higher rank and was sent to a "superior officer's course" in Santo Domingo. From there he was promoted to the rank of Lieutenant Colonel in 1924, the year the Americans left the island as occupiers; and he became Chief of Staff of the National Police. With his wily ways, Trujillo managed to induce the President to convert the National Police into an army brigade to which he became Commandant and finally, Commander in Chief of the Armed Services.

By way of a coup, political intrigues of the highest order and some of the usual strong-arm tactics, Trujillo was elected President of the Republic in 1930 and received diplomatic recognition from the United States. Two weeks after his taking office, a violent hurricane hit the capital which caused severe damage and more than two thousand deaths. Only the old colonial structures of solid coral rock several feet thick built by the Spanish more than four centuries before remained standing. Trujillo, with the help of American charities, took control of the situation and emerged as a leader the people looked up to. Now, with political control as well as control of the military, he looked to gain even more power by taking over some of the big business interests in the country. One of the properties he acquired was a large area to the east of Puerto Plata on the north shore which had belonged to the United Fruit Company. The American company had sold its interests years before and the land had become vacant with only five clapboard buildings remaining to mark the site together with a beautiful beach nestled within its protective cove. This would become the area destined for the Jewish refugees caught up in the insanity of the Holocaust, but there is more to the story as to Trujillo's motives.

In his first term as President, Trujillo had to face the problem of thousands of Haitians crossing the border to squat on Dominican soil. Relations with neighboring Haiti had never been good since the brutal Haitian occupation of the Dominican Republic in the early 19th century and the Haitian attempt to obliterate Dominican culture in order to dominate the eastern two-thirds of the island with its fertile land. Dominican Independence is dated from 1844, the year the Republic was created and the Haitians were driven back to their own borders.

Haiti in the 18th century had been the richest colony of the Americas: sugar, coffee, cacao. The French colonial planters pushed the envelope to the maximum by deforesting and clearing the land for their plantations and bringing thousands of African slaves to work the land. By the time Haiti had gained its independence during the Napoleonic period, the land had become completely exhausted and the slave population had grown considerably. This burgeoning populace, without an agricultural land base to cultivate, looked desperately to the Dominican side of the island and invaded with the intention to remake the entire island as their own. The Dominicans suffered every indignity imaginable during this occupation and the enmity brought about by this invasion still remains tucked away within the Dominican psyche of today.

In 1934, as Haitian squatters had once again crossed the border and confusion was brought about by an unclear mapping of the border in certain places, Trujillo's government formed a commission with the Haitian government to officially come to an understanding to confirm the border situation. By 1935, the commission had come to its conclusion and there was an official agreement as to the border line. Attempts to uproot the Haitian squatters lingered on for two more years and diplomatic complaints did nothing to resolve the situation. Finally, an altercation broke out between Dominicans and Haitians over the ownership of land near the border and several Dominicans were killed. Old and new enmities flared and the Dominican response in October of 1937, was a massacre of thousands of Haitians throughout the Republic. Horrible stories surfaced from the massacres, yet leading newspapers in the United States paid little attention to the problem and Washington made no public protest and no action was taken against the Dominican government. This was the time when America found itself in the worst throes of the Depression and we were going through an introspective nightmare which largely precluded interest in events occurring in other countries. The American Secretary of State, Cordell Hull, however, became distinctly unfriendly towards the Trujillo regime; and this presented itself as a problem to the Dictator. Although the Dominican Republic is a sovereign country, there had been an element of American sanction to Dominican actions and policies, especially since the American occupation of the country a dozen years before; and, here, Trujillo had gone too far.

Cordell Hull, the American Secretary of State

American-trained, grateful for American recognition of his Presidency and grateful for American aid after the dreadful hurricane of 1930 and, now, looked upon with disfavor by the American State Department, Trujillo, as the voice of the government, looked to regain his special recognition with the United States. It is most probably for these reasons that he made his offer at the Evian Conference of '38 in the form of 100,000 Dominican visas and resettlement land in the village of Sosúa, which had been the parcel of land of the United Fruit Company, to Jewish refugees looking to escape from Europe.

This was a most welcome gesture as viewed by President Roosevelt, as all the other governments at the Conference had voiced sympathy for the plight of the refugees, but none had been willing to accept them. In the United States, immigration quotas, depression and the fear of competitiveness in the few jobs to be had, outright anti-Semitism within the State Department and the general populace at the time, plus the pervading opinion that Europe should take care of its own problems had tied President Roosevelt's hands to be able to regulate any increased flow of refugees into the United States. There was also a paranoid fear of importing "fifth-columnists" into

the country in any great emigration, which was no small factor. Anyone who has seen the Hitchcock thriller "Saboteur" with Robert Cummings and Priscilla Lane, knows how real the terrorist threat was at the outbreak of the War. Dr. Chaim Weizmann, who would become Israel's first President in 1948, was quoted as saying, "The world seemed to be divided into two parts—those places where the Jews could not live and those where they could not enter." The fact that President Trujillo was able to make the offer at Evian was also founded on the appreciable lack of anti-Semitism among the Dominican population as a whole.

As an outgrowth of the Evian Conference, American Jewish aid organizations were formed to implement the resettlement with DORSA, the Dominican Republic Settlement Association, created to acquire the land, administer the funds donated by the parent organizations and to act as the representative of the refugees vis-à-vis the Dominican government and, also, as the settlers' governing body. Official studies launched by the State Department to investigate how the land could be used only served to delay the whole process and by the time the War had broken out in Europe, the refugees' precarious situation had taken a backseat to the overwhelming scenario of the war effort itself. Because of this bureaucratic delay, there were only some five hundred refugees who finally made it to Sosúa to settle the area; but as a result of the more than 5,000 Dominican visas issued during this period, many more were able to flee from the Holocaust.

ALONG THE NORTH SHORE, about fifteen miles to the east of Puerto Plata, lies the little town of Sosúa with its beautiful beach of palms and white sand. Columbus had taken note of it on his first voyage to the New World. Three blocks from the beach, in the center of town, stands a small clapboard building surrounded by a garden gate bearing the star of David. This is the little synagogue built

in 1941 by the Jewish refugees who came to the area to settle and work the land because of the magnanimous offer of President Trujillo at the Evian Conference. It is probably the only synagogue to have been built in 1941 in all the world and has been lovingly cared for throughout the years. Built completely of wood with the sanctuary as its only room, the building serves as a religious school and a social gathering hall as well as for religious services. In a time when contemporary American synagogues tend towards the grandiose, it seems like a pleasant, warm bit of nostalgia to experience this simple little temple of spirituality which relates so well to its surroundings. It stands as a symbol of hope from a time when despair seemed overwhelming for Jews in war-torn Europe. The interior is laid out in the Sephardic arrangement with the pulpit facing the ark and flanked by benches of polished pine. Simple jalousie windows from above ventilate and provide light into the sanctuary. Sephardic Jews trace their ancestry back to medieval Spain whereas the Ashkenazi Jews take their origins from Germany and Eastern Europe. To the right of the synagogue is the recently reopened Jewish Museum of Sosúa which chronicles the settlement of the town.

The beautiful beach at Sosúa

The little synagogue of Sosúa

Most of the settlers arrived in the years 1940–41, when it was still possible to get out of German held territories with foreign visas and a great deal of luck, but without any property. Over the years I have had the privilege of meeting a few of the original settlers and of hearing their stories. When they originally came to Sosúa, there was no native population; the only buildings were the five clapboard buildings left by the United Fruit Company years before and there were no roads connecting to any of the nearby towns. Because of the community's isolation—a paved road to any nearby town was not a reality until 1980—the settlers had to create some measure of self sufficiency and developed their own water works, sanitation system, clinic, school, shops and synagogue. Landlocked, they began their collective agricultural community with the cultivation of small produce: cabbage, beets, carrots and other greens. After eking out a subsistence existence, they eventually went into the business of cattle ranching; and because of barriers in communication and delivery in those days of the Dominican Republic, they developed systems for processing their meat and dairy products to prolong shelf life so they could market their products throughout the country. From this developed the large industry of sausage and cheese under the name of *"Productos Sosúa"* which has become a major economic player of the industries in the area.

One of the original settlers was Arturo Kircheimer, a spry gentleman of 80 years, who took me out to visit his *finca* (ranch). Originally from Hamburg, don Arturo worked in fabrics in a large department store there. It had been his first job and he had worked diligently to make some kind of future out of it. A few years after Hitler had come to power, the store began letting their Jewish employees go one by one because of the political pressure at the time; Arturo was the last to go. Fortunately, he was able to get out of Germany and make it to Luxemburg; and from there, to France where he was able to work at odd jobs until the German occupation. When the Germans entered

The refugees' arrival in Santo Domingo (above) and in Sosúa (below)

(Both photos courtesy of the Jewish Museum of Sosúa)

France, he was taken to a concentration camp near Bayonne which was only a temporary transit stop, as from there, the people were sent to the camps in Poland. One of the agents from DORSA had visited the camp and, luckily for Arturo, made provision for him to come to Sosúa by way of a Dominican visa and the funds necessary to make the trip. This brought on a wellspring of hope, but there was still a big hurdle to go. 1941 was the year the German High Command had begun to severely limit Jewish emigration out of the Reich, especially for those of working age. The Gestapo had especially looked to implement the policy and gave the orders denying further emigration. The SS, however, was in charge of the camps; and because of an ongoing rivalry and mistrust between the SS and the Gestapo, the SS Commandant of the camp decided to honor the Dominican visas and illegally abetted the escape of Arturo and 50 others to leave on a freighter bound for the Americas out of Marseilles. He arrived in Sosúa in early summer, 1941.

don Arturo

Martín Katz was a young man in his early twenties who was working on the railroad in a small village just north of Düsseldorf. As a country boy, he was familiar with the ways of farm life and his work

don Martín

at the railyards was a demanding one. Luckily, he was put in touch with a DORSA agent who extended him a Dominican visa in 1940; and because of the worsening conditions after the outbreak of the War, he used his railroad connections to make it to the Italian border and, finally, to the port of Genoa. Although Italy was aligned with Germany, fighting had yet to be a factor in Italy at that time. He recounts how he had to spend three days in Genoa, with hardly any money, while awaiting the ship bound for the Americas. But he arrived in Sosúa in early 1940 as one of the first settlers in the community.

The Jewish community of Sosúa, albeit small, live in harmony with their surroundings. Although many of the settlers emigrated to the United States after the War, those who remained, and the émigrés, too, are so very grateful for the Dominican offer at Evian, which was in reality, President Trujillo's offer at Evian. They are all proud to share their stories and proud of the Dominican Republic. All the objections put forth by other governments at the Conference proved to be unfounded. The Jewish settlers *did* take to working the land and proved not to be any drain on the local economy. Quite to the contrary, they formed industries which are, in large part, the mainstay of the local economy. They also intermingled with the native population through trade partnerships and marital unions; but they were always careful to preserve and respect their Jewish traditions. This is the miracle of Sosúa and a glorious chapter in the history of the Dominican Republic.

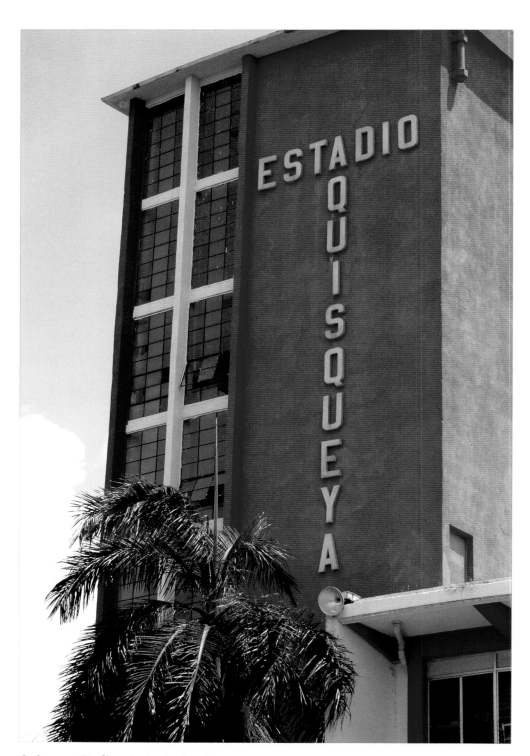

Quisqueya Stadium in Santo Domingo

6. El Béisbol

WHEN A TRAVELER from the States arrives in Santo Domingo during the American baseball season, a cab driver or the man in the street will often want to talk about what is going on stateside in the great American sport. Dominicans love baseball; they have a passion for it and they are well represented in the major league teams in the U.S. and Canada. Sammy Sosa, Alfonso Soriano, Pedro Martínez, Manny Ramírez, Vladimir Guerrero, Albert Pujols, Miguel Tejada, Alex Rodríguez, Ozzie Virgil, the Alou brothers, Tony Peña and Hall of Famer Juan Marichal are, without question, some of the best baseball players in the world; and they all hail from the Dominican Republic. In fact, the 2004 rosters of the major leagues included 79 Dominicans, nearly ten percent of the total roster, while the minors have about 25 percent of their number with young Dominican players under contract. Second only to the United States, the Dominican Republic produces more major league baseball players than any other country on the globe. This is an amazing fact and certainly qualifies as a present-day glory of the D.R.

Waiting for the game to begin

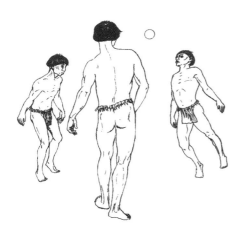

The game of pelota

How does a country of about nine million people produce so much baseball talent? How is it that non-Dominican major leaguers look to play baseball in the Dominican Winter League? Why has every major league team in the States invested in scouting and training young recruits in the Dominican Republic?

Even before the arrival of Columbus, *Taíno* boys were playing *pelota,* a ball game in which they would use their upper bodies to project a ball made of fiber, held together with resin from some of the fruit trees. They could not use their hands or feet and would play in a central square called a *batey.* This was one of their main activities when they were not learning to hunt and fish with their fathers.

Today, young, indigent descendants of these *Taíno* boys take folded milk cartons which they fashion into mitts, sugar cane stalks or broom handles or tree branches for bats and any small object that can be batted around for the venerable *béisbol.* Pedro Martínez, the famous pitcher who spent seven seasons with the Boston Red Sox, mentions that the boys would even pluck their sister's doll head when nothing else was available to get the game going, which generally got them into big trouble with their mothers.

If the Dominican Republic produces so much baseball talent, the hub of much of that talent is the old port city of San Pedro de Maco-rís, about fifty miles to the east of Santo Domingo. Dominican super-stars like Sammy Sosa, Manny Ramírez, Joaquín Andújar, Tony Peña, José Rijo, the Alou brothers, Manny Mota, George and Juan Bell and many others hail from San Pedro. And there may be several reasons for San Pedro's predominance.

Baseball caps on the Calle Duarte

Historically, we noted in the first chapter how the *Macorix,* a fierce, aggressive native tribe, had made inroads into the area of San Pedro and further north into the area of the provincial capital of San Fran-cisco de Macorís even before the arrival of Columbus. The native *Taínos* had to hold their ground against these aggressive newcomers. It is curious to note that both these towns have teams in the Dominican

league: San Francisco has *los Gigantes del Cibao,* the Giants of Cibao, and San Pedro has the famous *Estrellas Orientales,* the Eastern Stars.

San Pedro de Macorís

As I wander the streets of San Pedro, I am struck by the glaring contrasts: elegant buildings that give testimony to San Pedro's importance as a commercial and cultural center at the turn of the twentieth century versus the present-day, stark poverty which seems ubiquitous. Half the streets are paved, and half are dirt roads that can become quite a mess after a heavy rain. Along the river are handsome buildings with elegant facades which probably served as business and accounting offices for the massive sugar refineries and their port; also on the banks of the river, ramshackle shacks of makeshift materials provide shelter for people living on the fringes. Playing *béisbol* and displaying some talent is often the way a boy can earn the money

needed to help his family overcome such dire conditions; and the fact that the sport is imbued within the boys at a young age adds to the mix. In San Pedro, even at birth, if it is a girl, a pink ribbon is put on the crib and if a boy, a baby baseball mitt.

The introduction of baseball into the Dominican Republic from the United States began in the late 19th century with the refinery owners' attempt to give the cane cutters and refinery workers some diversion from their repetitive hard labors. Wherever the cane fields and the refineries existed, so followed the introduction of what would become the great American sport. In San Pedro and San Francisco, in Jaina, just to the west of Santo Domingo, in Santiago and in La Romana, baseball became established as *the* form of diversion and the tableau for competition among the different refineries. *Sugarball,* a wonderful book on the history of Dominican baseball by Alan Klein, underlines the inseparable connection between the sugar industry and the development of the sport in the Dominican Republic. Cutting the cane with a machete prepares the arm strength and the stamina to bat or throw a ball with tremendous power, and San Pedro de Macorís was the center of the sugar industry at this time. The fact that work in the fields and the refineries was so hard, and with low wages at that, made the path of escape through baseball even brighter.

In the early 20th century, teams were becoming organized, and the competition began in earnest. The sport grew rapidly after the American occupation in 1916, catching up with baseball's development in such places as Panama, Cuba and Puerto Rico. By the 1920s, the level of sophistication and the obvious local talent made the D.R. one of the stops on the Caribbean circuit. Dominican players would play against other members of the circuit: Puerto Rico, Cuba, Venezuela and Mexico. Eventually, team owners from these other Latino countries began to sit up and take notice of the special Dominican prowess, and in time Dominican players were recruited to play on teams in these other countries as well. By the 1930s, however,

Dominican teams were holding their own against the others and had even begun to recruit talented black players from the Negro leagues in the U.S., the great Satchel Paige being one of the first, as well as Latino players from other countries.

This professional frenzy culminated in the season of 1937, which saw a wild thirty-six game series among the Dragons of Ciudad Trujillo (Santo Domingo), the Eagles of Santiago and the Eastern Stars of San Pedro. Politics, Trujillo-style, big money invested to bring in the best talent from other countries and an emotional crowd that witnessed the highest caliber of baseball together with theatrics on and off the field made the '37 season a high-water mark in Dominican baseball to that point. The Dragons won the day but left professional baseball in the D.R. at a standstill. The expense of the season, Trujillo's political troubles with the Haitian situation, deepening economic depression and the menace of war brought an end to professional baseball in the country until the 1950s. Yet the amateur games went on in the pure spirit of love for the game, with the local communities forming an especially strong bond with their teams. "The majority of the good players came from the sugar mills of San Pedro," according to Cuqui Córdova, probably the most famous baseball historian in the D.R. They were poor and hungry and put more enthusiasm into it.

The 1950s saw the development of a Professional Baseball Commission for the Dominican Republic, the crossing of the color line for professional baseball in the States and Castro's revolution in Cuba, which essentially took many of the good Cuban players out of the baseball scene. From the mid-1950s to 1980, Dominican baseball came of age, and working relationships were established with major league teams in the States. The Los Angeles Dodgers, the Pittsburgh Pirates, the Toronto Blue Jays and the San Francisco Giants were the first teams to avail themselves of the mother lode of talent in the Dominican Republic. Early on, players like Ozzie Virgil, the three

Alou brothers and Juan Marichal piqued interest in Dominican players so that scouts from all the major league teams began to eye with interest any potential talent in the country.

To place itself in sync with the baseball season in the States, the Dominican Commission even changed the Dominican professional season from summer to winter so that, after the World Series, ballplayers could avail themselves of the temperate winters in the D.R. and continue to play ball. The Winter League season would begin in late October and run through the beginning of February. There are six teams at present: Santo Domingo has two, *los Tigres de Licey* (the Tigers of Licey) and *los Leones del Escogido* (the Lions of the Chosen). Santiago has *las Águilas del Cibao* (the Eagles of Cibao); San Pedro de Macorís, *las Estrellas Orientales* (the Eastern Stars); San Francisco de Macorís, *los Gigantes del Cibao* (the Giants of Cibao);

and La Romana, *los Azucareros del Este* (the Sugar Workers of the East). The teams play a sixty-game schedule with a round-robin playoff, and the two finalists compete against the champions of the Caribbean Series from Puerto Rico, Venezuela and Mexico.

Until the 1970s, scouts from all the major league teams together with local scouts, many of them nothing more than glorified hustlers, would seek out boys with "talent," sign them up and bring them in for tryouts. In the years before the Dominican government stepped in to regulate the scouts, there were widespread abuses, especially with the local recruiters, but with greater commitment from the major league teams, academies were established in the late 1970s and early 1980s. The first academy was developed just north of Santo Domingo by the Toronto Blue Jays, while one of the larger ones, *Campo Las Palmas,* was built east of the capital by the Los Angeles Dodgers. The academies are

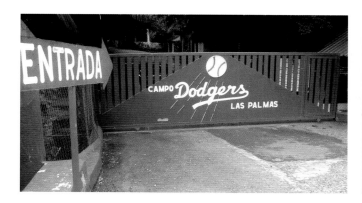

compounds with major league playing fields, dormitory facilities and a staff paid for by the major league teams. Here, boys of age 17 and older are given tryouts and, if accepted, are signed up for a thirty-day evaluation period, during which time they are sized up physically and emotionally by the staff and taught some of the basic skills of the game. This is an anxiety-producing period for the boys as the staff decides at the end of the thirty days whether to extend contracts or to send them back to their families. At the end of the evaluation period, those lucky enough to be accepted sign contracts and become rookies and play against other rookie teams within a system affiliated with the American minor league teams. Those who do not make the grade may try again after another thirty-day period has elapsed.

Meanwhile, amateur baseball is well organized throughout the twenty-six provinces of the Republic, with each having an association to oversee the play. The Dominican government plays a significant role in subsidizing amateur baseball and pays for instructors to teach the boys the basics of the game as well as paying for buses, park maintenance and lighting. Some of the wildest and most heated contests center around the refineries in the area of San Pedro de Macorís. Refinery teams from *Quisqueya, Porvenir* and *Consuelo* are continu-

ally playing one another, and the games are often attended by scouts from the major league teams. The scouts know this is fertile ground for future prospects. Some of the parks may be tumbledown and have dilapidated, makeshift stands; but the game is played wholeheartedly and with a verve that is a phenomenon in and of itself. I find the amateur games an extremely pleasant way to spend an afternoon. The boys, ages 13 to 17, play in the true spirit of the game and share a camaraderie which is at once obvious. Once immersed in the game, I feel as if I come to know something of each player's personality, and in a way, I begin to share their triumphs and defeats. It is baseball "up close." Watching the teams from the academies is also a treat; but here, it is almost like watching professional baseball itself. A throw from third to first occurs with lightning speed, and the pitching—the pitching can leave the spectator speechless.

During the Winter League season beginning in late October, Dominican superstars from the major leagues are often joined by non-Dominicans from the majors. However, since the advent of "free agency" in the States in the late 1970s and the lucrative contracts the teams have signed with the television networks, the Dominican superstars from the majors are making such astronomical salaries that they are less inclined to play in the Winter League. To avoid the risk of injury, they often confine their play to exhibitions or to token appearances in regulation play. Many Dominicans view this as a betrayal of cultural pride, but they do understand the issue of the big money.

While we in the States are super-saturated with professional sports—baseball, basketball, football and hockey, with the seasons overlapping one another—baseball is *the* sport in the D.R. So much cultural pride is infused in this one sport that it has become, in a way, a centerpiece for intercultural relations between the United States and the Dominican Republic. The fact that Dominicans can compete and excel in the major leagues is a source of pride for all Dominicans, even for those who are not fans of the sport. As Manny Mota,

former outfielder for the Los Angeles Dodgers, put it: "If you ask any Dominican what he is proudest of, he will read you a list of ballplayers. This country doesn't have much, but we know we are the best in the world at one thing [baseball]. That's not bragging, because it's true. And we plan to continue being the best in the world at it." While I tend to disagree with Manny with reference to the country's not having much, the fact remains that the great American sport is as entrenched in the Dominican Republic as rum and bananas; and proportionately, the Dominican Republic produces more major league players than any other country in the world.

To young Dominican boys, the baseball diamond often looms as a field of dreams. They know that their heroes all began under the same indigent circumstances as they did, and their dreams have the power to lift them up out of their dire circumstances into a brighter future. Even for those who do not make it, there is always the next month's tryouts and the shared pride in others from their own group who do make it. Hope is a precious commodity, and for so many Dominican boys, it is made possible through the great American sport. *¡A la pelota!* Let's play ball!

7. Dominican Cigars

THE DOMINICAN REPUBLIC is the largest producer and exporter of fine hand-made cigars in the world. It was the first place in the world to cultivate tobacco for commercial purposes, and it continues with a proud tradition to produce the greatest selection of premium cigars available for the cigar aficionado of today.

The center of tobacco cultivation is located in the heartland of the Republic, the *Cibao* valley, just north of the city of *Santiago* in the towns of *Navarrete* and *Tamboril*. This is the area that for many Dominicans represents the very heart and soul of the country for its fertility and for the intimate attachment the *campesinos,* the country folk, have to the land they cultivate. This was the land that Columbus first viewed with such awe on his journey from *Isabela* to *Jánico* in 1494, and that inspired him to give thanks to God for its great beauty and fertility. In fact, it was Columbus who first observed the *Taínos* smoking tobacco loosely rolled in a large tobacco leaf and through a tube called a *tobago* from which the name is derived.

The old tobacco museum of Santiago

"I believe that smoking contributes to a somewhat calm and objective judgment in all human affairs.

—ALBERT EINSTEIN

"If I cannot smoke in Heaven, I shall not go!"

—MARK TWAIN

EVERYONE TODAY is aware of the addictive nature of nicotine and the harmful effects that toxins in the tobacco smoke have on our health. But for those who enjoy a good cigar now and then, that complex balance of concentration and relaxation is a highly pleasurable experience; and the fact that some of the greatest creative minds of our time have been cigar smokers leaves the field open for thought. Anything to excess—food, water, even oxygen—can have harmful effects to our health as well, and in this respect, smoking is no different from any other excess. Twain, Hemingway, Churchill, Groucho, W. C. Fields and George Burns were avid cigar smokers. George Burns was reputed to have polished off ten *El Productos* a day between his remembrances of the good ole days of vaudeville and stories of Gracie's family, and he lived to be a hundred years old.

Physiologically, as a physician, I can understand some of this relaxation phenomenon from smoking with an analogy to the activity of *conscious breathing.* In conscious breathing, we distance ourselves from our world and concentrate on deep, rhythmic inhalations and exhalations which expand the stretch receptors in the lung tissue and promote the release of endorphins, those pleasurable neurotransmitters in the brain. This is why taking a deep breath when things become hectic is often a way of returning to equilibrium. Smoking also promotes these mechanisms with the additional aroma and flavor of the tobacco itself. I remember as a child in elementary school, before the age of plastics and gross mass consumption, we would

gather our school supplies—crayons, rounded scissors, school paste, pencils—and we would put them all into a cigar box to hold them. How vividly I remember opening the box any number of times just to smell the captivating aroma of the cigars.

On a recent trip to the Dominican Republic, I had the opportunity of meeting *don Leonel Díaz Bomnín*, a Cuban expatriate of five years who was a university professor of tobacco cultivation in Cuba before emigrating to the D.R. Don Leonel, an amiable gentleman in his early fifties, began to fill me in on some of the complex variables that go into the growing of a premium tobacco. He admits that climatic conditions, in terms of temperature and humidity, may be a little better in his native Cuba; but he says, the soil in the Cibao Valley near Santiago is superior to any other. Rich in potassium, calcium carbonate and organic matter; the soil approaches the right balance of acidity and the nutrients that the young tobacco plant requires in its rapid growth. But, as don Leonel is quick to add, it is *man* who makes the difference in a premium tobacco. It is the artistry and technology that man puts into the mix that makes the difference between an ordinary harvest and a premium one. The right seeds, the soil appropriate to the strain of the seeds, the additional nutrients at the right time in the plant's growth, the constant vigilance concerning temperature and humidity: all this and more bring about a premium tobacco. It must be harvested, dried, stored and allowed to ferment, all under the watchful eye of the artisan.

The arrival of Cuban immigrants following Castro's revolution was a shot in the arm to the production of premium tobaccos in the Dominican Republic. There had been quality production before, but now the technology and the human factor were greatly amplified. This effect shows in the diverse brand names that echo their Cuban origins. Yet the pure strains brought from Cuba have been greatly increased over the years, so that while Cuban premium tobaccos come from three or four varieties, there are now more than twelve pure

strains of premium tobaccos grown within the Republic. This allows for a greater choice in the final blends that make up the intricate aromas, flavors and character of the numerous brands of fine cigars. Manufacturers like Arturo Fuente, Litto Gómez, Flor Dominicana, Augusto Reyes and many others are producing a wide assortment of premium cigars that are attracting more and more aficionados as the new blends become available.

To me, I find the tobacco plant very beautiful in its growth. Those who refer to it as a weed obviously belong to the anti-tobacco faction; but the plant itself, with its lush green foliage and its rapid growth, is very pleasing to look at. Few agricultural fields are so picturesque as a tobacco field in the sun. The plant grows from a sprig a few inches high to about five feet over the course of six to eight weeks. This rapid growth drains the soil of nutrients, and constant vigilance is needed to provide additional minerals and fertilizer. The greener the plant, the more chlorophyll it is making, which in turn relates to the amount of nitrogen it is receiving, and there is an optimal carrier of nitrogen for each strain of tobacco. Phosphorus in a favorable ratio to the nitrogen; potassium to build carbohydrate and protein and act as a

carrier for other minerals; calcium, secondary only to nitrogen for growth; the additional minerals magnesium, boron, manganese, aluminum, sulfur and iron—all these must be provided in optimal amounts to the young plant in order to harvest the highest premium tobacco possible.

The growing season in the Cibao Valley extends from early November to the beginning of March. The crop is harvested with only the top leaves destined for inclusion in premium tobaccos. The leaves are hung up to air-dry in open huts in the field for six weeks and then placed in layers, hydrated and covered in burlap to allow for fermentation. Depending on the frequency of continued layerings, the tobacco acquires a mild, medium or stronger flavor. The leaves are then sorted as to size and integrity and subjected to more fermentation. Finally, they are placed in bales of approximately 120 lbs. and covered in burlap, stored under strict conditions and allowed to age from 2 to 6 years before they reach the hands of the master blender. The fermentation process and the time the leaves are allowed to age are proprietary and highly guarded secrets of the cigar masters, and they account for the distinct aromas and flavors of the end products.

As the filler, binder and wrapper reach the assembly stage, there is an even tighter quality control and personal evaluation for each of the distinct brands in the Dominican Republic. The final product is

ready to be rated as to its construction, its draw upon being lit, the aggressiveness of the smoke (how it feels on the tongue and throat), its burning qualities and the character of its body, flavor and aroma. The end product must have that special appeal to the senses: the visual, the sense of smell, feel and taste.

Tobacco cultivation and cigar production in the Republic employ a good number of people; and from what I have seen, the workers take a great deal of pride in their work and seem highly committed. Don Leonel tells me that associations of growers and blenders are forming to keep the highest premium quality in Dominican cigars. Whether the reader is a cigar aficionado or not, the pride and tradition, the quality control, the artistry and the technology of the Dominican tobacco industry are, indeed, another modern-day glory of the Dominican Republic.

La Aurora: one of the best for 2005, according to **Cigar Aficionado** *magazine*

131

Afterword

Travel through the Dominican Republic can be very exciting and richly rewarding, but there are times when a traveler needs the spirit of adventure and the *chutzpah* of an Indiana Jones to get the most out of his/her experience. Also, a rudimentary understanding of Spanish is a must in the cities and within the countryside; English is spoken in the resort areas and most of the larger hotels, but you need to speak and understand Spanish to some degree. The natives are friendly and hospitable and will always try their best to understand what you are trying to say and to guide you in the right direction; but a word of caution. While superhighways and fast foods are few and far between, American cable TV and young Dominicans returning from the U.S. have had some effect on this island paradise. Wandering the cities at night without the knowledge of where you are going is no longer a safe practice, especially if you are alone. Use common sense and be able to say "no" if you harbor any suspicions; but, keep in mind, Santo Domingo is generally safer than any American city its size.

All the pictures in this book were shot using film without enhancements or modifications. The spectacular beauty of the land, its people and its monuments really speak for themselves, and I envy anyone who is about to embark on a personal "discovery" of this enchanted land of the Dominican Republic.

Architectural Terms

ARCHITECTURAL TERMS may seem confusing to follow at times, but with a simple, overall look at the different periods in history, they become easy to recognize and add a special enjoyment to the periods they represent. They not only reflect the aesthetic trends of the time, but also, they indicate advances in engineering and building materials as well as sociopolitical changes which took place during those same periods.

Think of the different architectural styles along a time line.

Romanesque	Gothic	Renaissance
1000–1200	1200–1500	1500–1600

The *Romanesque* style came into being from the turn of the first millennium until about the year 1200. During these turbulent times, there were no central governments and the people had aligned themselves with the nobles who had jurisdiction over their respective domains. The one unifying force in the world at that time was the

Church which assumed its role through the institution of three important factors: the adoption of the Latin rite for the Mass, the adoption of the Gregorian calendar which standardized the holy feastdays and the adoption of a so-called, new form of architecture, the Romanesque. By standardizing this new architecture, a Christian could identify with other Christians even if he/she made pilgrimages to holy sites far from home. The *Romanesque,* "Roman-like," was a style taken from the old Roman basilica. The walls were heavy to maintain structural integrity, the buildings low to the ground, intimate with its surroundings. The rounded arch, which was the most notable characteristic of the Romanesque, was the strongest support as conceived by the ancient Romans and its heavy use in buildings, bridges and aqueducts is evident throughout the ancient world. The churches of the Romanesque period had very small windows because all the weight of the building centered upon its thick, heavy walls and, consequently, Romanesque churches often served as places of refuge for the people in times of trouble. And, because the populace could neither read nor write during these times, biblical stories were displayed graphically by way of carved images in stone on the capitals atop the columns or within the tympanums above the doorways. Romanesque sculpture told the story without any special emotional or decorative character to her figures. A good example of the Romanesque style is the church of San Stefano on page 41.

The *Gothic,* on the other hand, originated in 12th century France and was as different from the Romanesque as any two styles of architecture could be. Advances in building engineering and construction materials as well as the emergence of large cities and a new bourgeoisie to populate them brought about buildings which now soared into the heavens. The pointed arch now became the hallmark of Gothic architecture and the stress to support the great new towering buildings was taken off the walls and distributed more evenly onto

The beautiful Gothic cathedral of Burgos, Spain

flying buttresses and abutments and onto vaultings within the ceilings. This allowed the appearance of large areas of stained glass taking up much of the wall space in these structures. Gothic sculpture went along with the new architecture more as a decorative afterthought to complement the building style. There is very little emotional character to its figures and its stylization is intended to provide relief to the structure itself without much of a story-telling function. The *Isabelina* is a sub-style of the late Gothic period, 1480–1505, and coincides with the last half of Queen Isabel's reign in Spain. It is a more florid expression of Gothic elements—pointed arches with intricate filigrees within them—now, more decorative than functional. The Isabelina style eclectically took elements from other architectural expressions like Moorish tilework and Byzantine touches like the little globes which serve as a decorative border.

Isabelina window (florid Gothic), Manzanares el Real, province of Madrid, Spain

Renaissance architecture, like the Romanesque, takes its inspiration from classical antiquity, but now on a much grander scale. With the advances in building and engineering, this was made possible. The hallmarks of this impressive style were the elliptical arch and a new harmony in architectural expression by balancing the same elements on either side from center. Windows and accents mirror-imaged themselves from right to left. Buildings were grandiose and rather stark in and of themselves, but for two sub-styles which sought to adorn these classic structures—the *Plateresque* and the *Mannerist.* The Plateresque (silver-like) arose in early 16th century Spain as a special touch of elegant filigrees, vines and even classic human figures to grace the grand doorways and facades of Renaissance buildings. Its intricacies carved into the stone simulated the elegant work of the Muslim artisans of Toledo working their sumptuous patterns into the Damascene silver. The doorway into the Casas Reales highlights the Plateresque. The Mannerist sub-style arose later in 16th century Italy and included Cupids, acanthus leaves and vines as borders carved into stone or

The elliptical archways of the Renaissance, Manzanares el Real, province of Madrid, Spain

wood. The canopy bed in doña María's bedroom within the alcázar best delineates this sub-style of the Renaissance.

Renaissance sculpture, like the great paintings of the Renaissance, evolved to display poignant expression in the faces of its figures along with a more realistic proportion in their body shapes. If a character is sad or reflective, this can be easily seen in the face. Renaissance art takes its initial inspiration in the paintings of Giotto in the early 14th century and becomes more widespread as Renaissance architecture becomes the dominant style.

Bibliography

Arnaiz, Francisco Jose, S.J. *Más Luces que Sombras.* Collección Quinto Centenario, Santo Domingo, R.D., 1989. Interesting, fresh looks into the people and events of Dominican history from the beginning years. In Spanish.

Arzeno Rodríguez, Luis. *Trujillo . . . Chapita No!* Santo Domingo, República Dominicana, 1997. In Spanish.

Báez Díaz, Tomás. *Quinto Centenario* (colección), 1992. Santo Domingo, R.D.

Besio, Armando and Mario Paternostro. *Genoa.* Guide to the new and the old city, 1992. Edizioni Costa & Nolan. In English.

Bosch, Juan. *Indios.* Apuntes Históricos y Leyendas. 5ta edición, 2000. Editora Alfa & Omega, Santo Domingo, República Dominicana. In Spanish.

Dobal, Carlos. *Como pudo ser la Isabela.* Pontificia Universidad Católica Madre y Maestra, Santiago, República Dominicana. 1988. In Spanish.

Domínguez, Jaime de Jesús. *Historia Dominicana,* 2001. Abc editorial, Santo Domingo, R.D. In Spanish.

Hazard, Samuel. *Santo Domingo, past & present with a glance at Hayti,* 3rd edition, 1982. Editora de Santo Domingo, S.A. Originally published in 1873 by Harper & Brothers, NYC. In English. Fascinating 19th century account of the island and its history.

Henríquez Ureña, Pedro. *Obra Dominicana.* 1988. Sociedad Dominicana de Bibliófilos, Inc.

Klein, Alan M. *Sugarball: The American Game, the Dominican Dream.* 1991. Yale University Press. A delightful historical and sociological work on the development of baseball in the Dominican Republic.

Liogier, Dr. Alain Henri. *Diccionario Botánico de Nombres Vulgares de la Española*. 2000. Jardín Botánico Nacional Dr. Rafael Ma. Moscoso, Santo Domingo, R.D.

Morison, Samuel Eliot. *Admiral of the Ocean Sea*. 1942. Little, Brown & Company. The Pulitzer Prize–winning history by the Harvard professor who gives the definitive, objective story of Columbus while including some of the passionate adventure of his life.

Moscoso Puello, Francisco. *Cartas a Evelina*. Editora Cole, Santo Domingo, R.D., 1era edición, 1941. Delightful series of essays in which the author, a Dominican physician and philosopher, comments on the realities and the foibles of his country and countrymen. For those who would delve into Dominican ways, this book is a "must." In Spanish.

Ortega, Elipidio José. *La Isabela y la Arqueología en la Ruta de Colón*. Universidad Central del Este, San Pedro de Macorís, y la Fundación Ortega Álvarez, Inc., 1988. Taller, Isabel la Católica 309, Santo Domingo, República Dominicana. In Spanish.

Palm, Erwin Walter. *Los Monumentos Arquitectónicos de la Española*. 1era edición, 1955. 3ra edición, 2002, Editora Manatí, Santo Domingo, R.D. Sociedad Dominicana de Bibliófilos. Classical, highly intellectual survey of architectural monuments of the island as seen in the 1940's and '50's.

Pérez Montás, Eugenio. *Casas Coloniales—Colonial Houses,* 1980. Museo de las Casas Reales Voluntariado del Museo de las Casas Reales. In English and Spanish.

Rood, Carlton Alexander. *A Dominican Chronicle,* 1991. An English language version of Dominican history with a somewhat Anglo-Saxon bias. Taller, Isabel la Católica 309, Santo Domingo.

Suárez Marill, Lic. Mario. *Santo Domingo Colonial, sus principales monumentos,* 2003. Fotografías, Chema Mariscal. Santo Domingo. Spanish and English versions available.

Velázquez, Carlos and Ureña, Alejandro. *El Merengue y la Bachata*. Galos Publishing, NYC. 2004. In Spanish.

Index